WOMEN AND RELIGION
A Reader for the Clergy

edited by
Regina Coll, C.S.J.

paulist press  *new york/ramsey*

The Publisher gratefully acknowledges use of excerpts from *A Hymn to Him* by Alan Jay Lerner and Frederick Loewe. Copyright © 1956 by Alan Jay Lerner and Frederick Loewe. Chappell & Co., Inc., owner of publication and allied rights throughout the world. International Copyright secured. All rights reserved. Used by permission.

Acknowledgements

Many people supported me in this project, but some have contributed more than I could ever repay. Let me say that without the help and encouragement of Helen Costello, Lillian Kennedy, Pat McKenna and Rosalie Carven and the excellent suggestions of John Mahoney, this book would never be.

Library of Congress
Catalog Card Number: 82-81196

ISBN: 0-8091-2461-0

Published by Paulist Press
545 Island Road, Ramsey, N.J. 07446

Printed and bound in the
United States of America

Contents

to

Danny and the two Brians

Introduction

This book grew out of a conviction that Christianity is about the business of bringing good news to the poor, setting free the captives, helping the blind to see and proclaiming the year of the Lord's favor. It also grew out of an awareness that this business of liberation can only be accomplished when all Christians, women and men alike, work together in dignity and freedom for the coming of the reign of God. It is, therefore, an attempt to bridge the gap which we perceive between women who have newly found their voices and men who are trying to open their ears. This is not to suggest that women have the answers to bestow upon men; it merely indicates that women have recently discovered and uncovered their own experiences and history which must be shared if we are to be able to collaborate in renewing the face of the earth.

Most of the books about women—and there has been an avalanche of them in the past twenty years—speak of women's experience and perform the vital task of opening women's eyes and lives to the possibility of a full humanity. But it is not always easy to listen to people who have shifted their self-definition and their world view; it is not always easy to hear and understand the message of prophets.

Some men do attempt to read feminist literature but they find themselves feeling left out, somewhat alien to the discussion. The language sounds foreign, the images appear strange and the symbols and metaphors are uncomfortable.

The authors of these essays are all feminists and have all gone through the stages of consciousness raising with varying degrees of resistance and pain. They have here set themselves to the task of making what is foreign, strange and uncomfortable just a little more understandable. They do not try to make it more comfortable.

This book is only a beginning, a primer of sorts for clergy who minister with and to women in challenging but growthful ways. It may, at times, be difficult to read because it is a call to conversion, and conversion is never easy. Long-held values and privileges must be examined and either affirmed or abandoned; moreover, conversion usually involves an urgency to share with others the piece of the good news which we have found.

SITUATING THE QUESTION

The Socialization of Women into a Patriarchal System

Regina Coll

Children often play games at closing one eye and then the other to see how their span of vision changes. Objects appear to move left or right ever so slowly; peripheral views are blocked out; blinking quickly causes the whole image to dance back and forth.

The game of one-eyed-looking might be an apt metaphor for the way we grownups sometimes view the world. Ordinarily, we look with both eyes, seeing in a three-dimensional way, but sometimes we take a one-eyed view. We close one eye, look around and see evil, pain, suffering and guilt. It appears as if nothing in the world is right, and we are aware that the reign of God has not come in its fullness.

Then we blink. We look through the other eye and see almost the same view but from a slightly different perspective. The world, at least those structures in which we have a vested interest, appears to be exactly as it should be. Traditional institutions such as the family, Church and government are seen as divine givens. It is almost as if we believe that what we have here and now is precisely what God wills. The institutions which define our lives are sometimes bestowed with almost divine qualities to such a degree that we forget that they are all human inventions created by men and women to facilitate their living together.

Peter Berger has given a sociologist's perspective on this phenomenon which might be helpful here.[1] According to

Berger, there are three identifiable phases in the socialization process: externalization, objectification and internalization. Together people construct their world. By physical and mental activities, by a continual outpouring of themselves, human beings construct their society. Then the social structures take on a life, a facticity of their own which is external to and outside of the human producers. Finally, human beings define themselves by the expectations of the society they have created. They internalize that reality and begin to define themselves and others according to the norms of that society.

These processes are not successive but rather ongoing and simultaneous.

Humanity has created institutions such as governments, ecclesial structures, schools and families, sometimes over a period of centuries. Those structures become so powerful that they no longer depend on the efforts of their creators for their being. They exist, it seems, of themselves and we become their prisoners. It is difficult not to internalize this world, not to define oneself in terms of the family, Church or government, even if the definition is by way of exclusion. For instance, we talk of ex-Catholics, former spouses, and anti-Communists.

The premise, then, from which I am working is that men and women together created the culture which we have inherited, and we, in turn, are recreating that culture on a daily basis. Nations, communities, churches, clubs, schools, even families have been organized by people, have evolved and changed over the centuries according to people's needs and can be changed and improved if people so desire. Women and men from all walks of life make significant and unique contributions toward the socialization of the members of any given society.

God has not given us specific blueprints for structuring society. It is we who must build up that society after listening to the words of God spoken to us through Scripture and the community and in the quiet of our own hearts. Our Christian heritage is a challenge to create and recreate the face of the earth; that same Christian heritage also enables us to face that creating and recreating with hope rather than fear.

The process of socialization is especially evident in the institution of the family. We are so defined in terms of the family and we have glorified the family to such a degree that we have forgotten that the family, as we know it, is a rather recent innovation.[2] Two hundred years ago, the family of which we speak as if it were a God-given reality did not exist. Childhood as a time of play and schooling did not exist. Motherhood, in its romanticized and sentimentalized form, did not exist.

But childhood, motherhood and family do exist and are important in our society and they do affect the way each generation socializes the next one.

Adults become the persons they are primarily through the relationships which fill their lives. Children, in a more dramatic way, develop in response to the relationships in their lives. Parents, siblings, friends, enemies—all help to form and mold them. The society in which they live determines, to a great degree, their character and personality. Children from homes where religion is a value tend to grow into religious adults; on the other hand, children who are abused often grow into violent adults.

Home

Socialization into expected gender roles begins very early. In hospital nurseries, we see small cards on a newborn's crib: Baby Boy Conroy or Baby Girl Schwartz. Why is it important to label infants according to sex? It cannot make any difference to the other babies, and certainly the relatives who stare in amazement at this new life know whether they have a boy or a girl. So we might conclude that the signal is being given to the nurses who care for the children so that they may begin from the very start to treat the boys differently from the girls.

Surveys indicate that, from birth, the bodies of girls are touched, caressed, and cuddled in a way different from that of boys. They are treated as though they are more fragile, more likely to fall apart; they are spoken to in a higher, softer voice. The decorations in a baby's carriage send clues to admiring friends and relatives as to how the baby is to be treated. Very often, mobiles for little girls are made of flowers or butterflies while those for boys might be airplanes, rockets or even boxing gloves.

The toys, games and stories of childhood also reinforce society's expectations. Dolls and tea sets, trucks and guns—we send strong, if silent signals to children about acceptable behavior. Different life skills are learned in the games that boys and girls play. Cowboys and Indians, baseball and football involve activity, adventure and teamwork; playing house or school is much more passive, quiet and solitary. One may learn the rudiments of parenting but one does not learn teamwork or how to win or lose when playing with a doll.

I am not proposing that we try to eliminate one kind of game or the other, nor am I advocating unisex toys and games. I do suggest, however, that if we created an environment in which a little boy might, without embarrassment, play with a doll, we might be fostering a softness and nurturance which we hope for in fathers. If playing with dolls is preparation for being a good mother, might not playing with dolls be a good preparation for being a loving father?

If little girls were encouraged to play the same competitive games and to engage in sports to the same degree that boys are, perhaps winning and losing and teamwork would be part and parcel of their formation. Perhaps, too, engagement in active sports would strengthen their bodies so that they no longer would be looked upon as "the weaker sex."

If we only name some of the stories of our childhood we can develop a good picture of the role models which were held up to boys and girls. Cinderella, Sleeping Beauty, Snow White, Rapunzel and Little Red Riding Hood—all are variations on one theme: a helpless woman need only wait patiently for a great strong man to rescue her. On the other hand, Jack and the Beanstalk, Sinbad the Sailor, and the Gingerbread Boy promise that life is an adventure, a challenge to be enjoyed. Slowly but surely stories contribute to the gender defined roles which are held open to children.

Men who are embarrassed when their sons or nephews act in a way that they judge to be "sissy" are sending unconscious messages to their wives and daughters. It may be cute for Susie to be a tomboy—it is even an indication that she is somehow superior to other mere girls. But for brother Tom it is another story. If he is soft and gentle, he is mocked for being just like a girl. Being a tomboy is a step up but being like a girl is definitely six or seven steps down. Little boys who act like girls are penalized in our society because we do not prize femininity as highly as masculinity.

Our families are the first to set up the parameters, to box us into expected gender roles. By the age four or five, every boy and girl knows what parents and other relatives reward and punish; they know what is expected of big boys and of Daddy's little girl.

When we label some behavior as masculine or as feminine, we do so because it is culturally perceived as such, not because it is masculine or feminine according to nature. Margaret Mead reported that behavior which was appropriate to men in one tribe was women's work in another.[3] Her work is among those which suggest that it is we ourselves who determine, to a large degree, what is appropriate behavior.

Maleness and femaleness are determined by our physiology; masculinity and femininity are cultural designations.

School

Schools also reenforce stereotypic gender roles. When children line up in school, the girls are usually on one line and the boys on another; they are set in teams against one another; chores are assigned according to sex. Money spent on boys' sports programs is often many times that spent on similar programs for girls. Teachers expect—even tolerate—more deviant behavior from boys than from girls.

The role models provided in the school structure are also significant. Two-thirds of all public school teachers are women while only two percent of all secondary school principals are women. We do not have to give speeches about who really is in charge.

Textbooks have greatly improved in the area of racial and

sexual considerations over the past decade. Gone are the days when Jane fearfully watched Dick climb the trees; gone too the history books which spoke of brave pioneers who brought their wives and children across the continent. Just as we are beginning to become aware of the history of blacks and their contributions to the history of our country, so we are becoming aware of the history of women and of their contributions to history.

The home and school have played major roles in determining the position of women in society; the Church, too, has made an impact. I will here discuss three aspects of the impact: the negative image of women in some Christian writings, selective criteria for sanctity and male images of God.

Church

Christianity has long upheld, at least in principle, the equality of men and women. Galatians 3 set the stage for the way Christians were to relate: "All baptized in Christ, you have all clothed yourselves in Christ, and there are no more distinctions between Jew and Gentile, slave and free, male and female, but all of you are one in Christ Jesus."

1. *Negative Images of Women*

On the other hand, the principles upheld by Jesus and in Scripture have not always been carried out in practice. We are still suffering the after-effects from the blatantly misogynous views of some of the Church Fathers and Doctors. Negative views abound in their writings but two will be sufficient here.

Augustine taught that "woman together with her husband is the image of God, so that the whole substance may be one image, but when she is referred to separately in her quality as a helpmate which regards the woman alone, then she is not the image of God."[4] Aquinas, centuries later, calls woman "defective and misbegotten, for the active power in the male seed tends to the production of a perfect likeness according to the masculine sex; while the production of a woman comes from defect in the active power, or from some material indisposition, or even from some external influence, such as the south wind, which is moist, as the philosopher observes."[5]

No one upholds these principles today but they were influential in determining the low esteem in which women were held and are still held. One has only to read the Vatican Declaration on the ordination of women to see that the arguments concerning the defective nature of women and their inability to image God are not dead. Sacramental signs, we are told, must represent what they signify by natural resemblance. "When Christ's role in the Eucharist is to be expressed sacramentally, there would not be this 'natural resemblance' which must exist between Christ and his minister if the role of Christ were not taken by a man; in such a case it would be difficult to see in the minister the image of Christ. For Christ himself was and remains a man."[6]

The Declaration seems to have lost sight of the crucial theological question, that is, whether the minister's resemblance to Christ resides in one's sexuality or in one's humanity.

2. *Selective Criteria for Sanctity*

In *Grace and the Human Spirit,* Juan Luis Segundo developed a critique of the *Imitation of Christ* and the kind of sanctity which it fostered for so long. Removal of oneself from the world, hatred of that world even, and a solitary relationship between a soul and God led to a privatized notion of sanctity and also a privatized notion of sin. This type of spirituality, for all its beneficial aspects, did little or nothing to focus on the causes of suffering of a great part of humanity. It did not call us to responsibility for our sisters and brothers throughout the world.[7]

The language associated with monasteries and convents created a further split between the sacred and the profane. There were those who had a "sacred calling" to the "higher life," who had a "vocation" to "religious life" and were themselves called "religious." Other Christians were the laity. This language suggested that, as a matter of fact, cloistering oneself from the world was a prerequisite for a truly holy life. The language, as all language, both described the dominant culture and reinforced its hold on society.

I suggest that in the case of women, the criteria for sanctity were even more restrictive of full human relationships. A search through the catalogue of saints reveals that even when women were canonized they were defined by their biology. Besides martyrs the vast majority of women saints are listed under the categories of virgin, widow, and the catch-all "neither virgin nor martyr." Even in Scripture, women are defined in relationship to a man. Women in the Bible are, ordinarily, someone's wife, mother or whore. This stress on a woman's sexuality has led to a negative and deficient theology of sexuality.

The Christian virtues most honored in women are passive, dependent, self-abnegating and other-oriented. Historically, since women existed for others, they were often treated as if they had no worth of their own; girl infants were devalued, young women were given or sold in marriage as chattel, and at times women were raped and abused with impunity.

While these conditions have improved in recent times, there are still remnants of these attitudes operative in our society and our churches. Women are not treated as full and equal members in society or in the Church. The Roman Catholic Church is particularly wanting in this area. Significant issues regarding women are discussed and decisions are made, often without the deliberative participation of women. The issue of human sexuality is a fine example of this. Celebate males unilaterally pronounce laws and rules for women to obey. Another instance is the current revision of Canon Law for religious congregations of women. This commission is exclusively composed of males; women are perpetual minors in ecclesiastic matters.

The significant questions here are: Is this situation so clearly and unambiguously the revealed will of God? Does the subjection of women grow out of a theological basis or rather out of political and economic needs? What advantages accrue to the Church in fostering a privatized notion of sanctity and of sin?

In our work toward bringing about the reign of God, we must often ask ourselves very difficult questions about the structures with which we are involved and to which we pledge our loyalty.

3. *Images of God*

The third theological theme I wish to investigate is the concept of God. We know through our experiences which reveal the Divinity to us. It is God's activity in our world which comprises revelation.

> What God does is precisely the thing that reveals [God]: "God is love." ... What we call the miracles of Jesus were in fact, as the Gospel tells us, signs: i.e., acts signifying something, acts that spoke in themselves and revealed who was doing them....The prophets were men [and women] with double vision, so to speak. In things that happened they saw signs of the one who was responsible for them. Through the prophets, the historical event revealed [God] who was acting in history.
>
> In these two examples, which are clearer than any that can be offered to us by the activity of the Spirit in the Church, we see that it is God's activity that reveals [God]. There is no grounding statement of teaching about God on the abstract plane of essences. God reveals [God] in and through [God's] activity.[8]

Women often do not recognize this activity of God in their lives because the metaphors most commonly used for the transcendent are male. The works of God and the divine qualities are ordinarily associated with men; we speak of God's wisdom, power, might, and strength and judgment. The traditional metaphors for God are Lord, King, Father and Judge. The one metaphor that might most appropriately be associated with women is also reserved to men. We know from experience that every human being is born of a woman, that it is the mother who is the life-bearer and who plays the most active role in the creation of life. Yet when the story of creation was written, the author had Eve born, as it were, of Adam. And so, even in the act of creation, Adam and God are more directly related and Eve's relationship with God is through the mediation of Adam.

The fact that God is usually referred to in male terms, despite all our protestations that God is beyond any sexual characterization, sets men in a different relationship with God than the one women enjoy. God is mediated more directly to men. Women, for the most part, have a male intermediary between themselves and God.

The question here is why the revelation of God is almost always spoken of in male terms. Why do we rely on male images? Does maleness really mediate divinity in a better way? Are there perhaps unexamined cultural reasons for this phenomenon? Might it be considered, even unconsciously, to be of some advantage to the Church or to society to hold women in this lesser position?

An ideology, according to the dictionary, is "a manner or the content of thinking characteristic to an individual group or culture." Theologians, sociologists and psychologists challenge us to investigate our unconscious mind-set which contributes to and colors all our ideas, to ponder the ideologies which undergird our thinking, and to critically examine the thinking characteristic to our culture.

It is obvious that everyone works out of some ideological base, whether it is articulated or not. It is better to acknowledge one's ideology and consciously attend to it and be responsible for its consequences. In that way one may examine the effect of the conclusions which are reached.

The question, then, is not whether our cultural heritage has an impact on our thinking, but what kind of impact the culture has and whether that impact ought to be modified in any way. Ideologies, unexamined, ordinarily operate to maintain the status quo. Human beings tend to be more comfortable when the circumstances of life are not disrupted by questioning their validity. And yet, once it is acknowledged that everyone works out of some ideological perspective, it becomes incumbent upon us to take on an attitude of questioning or suspicion regarding our own ideologies.

I would suggest that one of the ideologies operative in our culture is a sort of mitigated patriarchy. When we examine the reasons for some of our most basic ideas, it becomes apparent that the male (the father) is supreme and maleness is the norm, not only for humanity, but also for divinity. Patriarchy may have been appropriate in another time and place. However, in the light of anthropological, psychological and historic insights available to us, the tenets of patriarchy when still embraced are more rightly called sexism.

NOTES

1. Peter Berger and Thomas Luckman, *The Social Construction of Reality* (Garden City, N.Y.: Anchor Books, 1967).

2. Philippe Aries, *Centuries of Childhood* (New York: Random House, 1962).

3. Margaret Mead, *Male and Female* (New York: Dell, 1949).

4. Augustine, *De Trinitate* 7.7,10, quoted in Rosemary Radford Ruether, *Religion and Sexism* (New York: Simon and Schuster, 1974).

5. Thomas Aquinas, *Summa Theologica,* Question XCII, Article I.

6. *Declaration on the Question of the Ordination of Women to the Ministerial Priesthood* (Washington, D.C.: U.S. Catholic Conference, 1976) p. 12.

7. Juan Luis Segundo, *Grace and the Human Spirit* (Maryknoll, N.Y.: Orbis Books, 1973).

8. Juan Luis Segundo, *Our Idea of God* (Maryknoll, N.Y.: 1971) p. 46.

To Each (Her) Due: Women, the Church, and Human Rights

Padraic O'Hare

The social movement broadly designated as "feminism" is, and will become even more evidently in the future, the most profound and global shift in human relations of the modern era. It will not do to dismiss Western feminist movements as the preoccupation of the well-fed, or even to relegate feminism to a subset of a broader movement, sometimes designated "the revolution of rising expectations." For feminism is a "response to a crisis of consciousness created by modern technological society."[1] And, more fundamental than this, "feminism is railing against problems that are built into the human condition."[2]

For those American Catholics who love the universal, orderly, pious and culturally rich Catholicism of their youth and who truly love women, there is a special pathos in the collision of the Roman Catholic Church and theological feminism. There is no real sadness or irony either in the disputations of the true misogynist within our Church (of whom, sad to say, there are more than a few), or in the unambiguous advocacy of Catholic feminists, for whom the righteousness of the cause becomes a warrant to ignore the pain and confusion of so many Catholics. This essay is a wholehearted plea for the full realization of the human rights of women in the Catholic Church. And, though it is concerned primarily with the question of rights and only secondarily with the ordination question, such is the identity of these two questions that the author necessarily will advocate such a change in Church discipline as part of the large discussion of rights.

But despite the absolute conviction expressed here about the imperative demands of feminism on the Catholic Church, my view would not be fully communicated if this essay did not begin on a note of sadness for the pain which so profound a shift in Church life has caused and will continue to cause for so many traditional Catholics. Indeed, an unsentimental yet genuine sensitivity to such matters is, for me, the criterion of whether those who advocate profound shifts in the life of any religious community are false prophets who bedevil human history, or true agents of the painful yet inevitable growth by which we are reminded that "history is God's instrument for destroying all of our established securities."[3] Those who can demand great change, however transparent the righteousness of their cause, with little or no acknowledgment of or feeling for the alienation, psychic and spiritual confusion and anxiety with which their doctrine and demand are met by great numbers of those to whom it is addressed, show us nothing more than their own thin humanity, pride and self-indulgence. Those who, with equal rigor, approach their task with reverence for all those on whose ears the painful message will fall—those prophets know, as Reinhold Niebuhr has expressed it, that the realm of moral choice is the realm of "tragic choice." They know that religions arise among people precisely to bring consolation, confidence and a sense of order amidst the flux and loss that seem to accompany the passage of time.[4] And so, even as they challenge and bring pain to those (all of us in one way or another) who would resist the call to live for a kingdom not yet at hand, these people practice empathy, and they suffer with those for whom their message is one of pain.

The pained include traditional Catholic women, who are conscious of no oppression and marginalization, for whom the Church within which they grew up still nurtures and promotes a personal life of meaning, charity and peace. These women are often of a generation whom Elizabeth Moltmann-Wendel has described as that "well-balanced, controlled, friendly, seemingly sane generation. When they were asked whether they would like another cup of coffee, they said 'but only if you are getting up anyway.' "[5]

The pained include priests in the middle and older years who cherish a sentimental view of womanhood in the image of a recent Marian piety, but who never consciously harbored anti-feminine sentiment, and who indeed revere the virtue of women. These and other "types" in the Church possess a hopelessly uncritical view of the subjugation of women in the Church and in society. They know nothing of that woman whom Molt-mann-Wendel describes in this painful evocation:

> Women who seemed very independent but who fell silent as soon as they were with their husbands.... Sometimes they disclosed—mostly at a late and relaxed hour—what profession they had once wanted to enter; and what had filled them with enthusiasm and passion when they were young; a distinct personality then emerged from the anonymity of middle-class married. Yet if one encountered them the next day, they had fallen back into anonymity and were once again devoted functionaries of married and family life.[6]

Still less do these traditional Catholics know of less subtle physical and psychological brutalization of women that occurs and has occurred on a global level. Yet many of these are good people for whom—like ourselves—religion functions as an instrument of security and order.

The cause of theological feminism and its central and symbolic issue, ordination, has about it the character of a moral imperative; therefore, only a demonic sentimentality would stay the hand of those determined to see human rights respected in the Church. Still, only so profound an issue of humanity gives us leave to bring consternation and confusion in the Church. Let us do so in prayer and fasting, and with a healthy measure of sympathy!

Though the primary focus of this essay is human rights theory, the question of ordination is inevitable. I am more than a little suspicious of some women's motives for ordination advoca-cy, finding in such advocacy the echo of clerical elitism and a triumphal Church. Still, there is equal or greater cause for suspi-cion of the motives for ordination of many male candidates for the "clerical state." And one can be reassured by the assurances of some of the finest leaders of tbe Women's Ordination Move-ment in this country that the movement is about—among other things—the reform of the clerical state itself in favor of true priestly ministry. The ambiguity surrounding the relationship of the questions of ordination and human rights in the Church lies in the fact that ordination is at once only a symptom of the deeper problem of human rights, and yet it is the chief symbol and effect of this deprivation of rights. This ambiguity is com-pounded by a certain ennui in the face of theological and bibli-cal arguments about the legitimacy of "women's ordination," as if the self-evident were being subjected to vast, scholastic, dispu-tation. It is not that reasons drawn from the Bible and theology are disdained here. It is simply that the matter seems resolvable by appeal to "that self-evidence which sustains itself in civilized society."[7] Can one not appeal, in insisting on the eligibility for ordination of human beings who are women, to rational princi-ples of natural justice? R. S. Peters recapitulates this tradition by naming four such principles, written in our hearts (if, that is, we have had the good fortune to grow within reasonable communi-ties of people). These are: freedom, impartiality, reciprocity and respect for persons.[8] Could not Pope Pius XII's expression of the foundation for the common good and of the unity of human-kind serve as a rationale for so self-evidently fair a decision:

> . . . that law of human solidarity and charity which is
> dictated and imposed by our common origin and by the
> equality of rational natures and by the redeeming sacri-
> fice offered by Jesus Christ on the altar of the cross.[9]

This sense of the futility—and gratuity—of so much of the argument over ordination (and of the tortuous logic of the Ro-man document, "Declaration on the Question of the Admission

of Women to the Ministerial Priesthood")[10] grows more pro-
nounced when one in fact does turn to the testimony of biblical
and early Church origins.

As Rosemary Radford Ruether has pointed out, "a reading
of the Synoptic Gospels reveals a startling element of icono-
clasm toward the traditional subordination of women in Jesus'
life."[11] It is not surprising that Celsus could mock the new
Christian sect as a "religion of slaves and women." For Jesus'
close women friends accompanied him throughout his public
ministry, Jesus contrasts the faithfulness of a poor widow with
the faithless religious establishment, Jesus' first miracle is per-
formed at the behest of a woman, Jesus' doctrine of divorce is on
behalf of women's rights, women are the first witnesses to the
resurrection faith, women are prophets, women are missionaries, and one may have co-authored an epistle in the canon of
Scripture. Finally, it is likely that there were women serving
roles in the early Church reserved now for male priests.

As to the arguments advanced in the "Declaration on the
Question of the Admission of Women to the Ministerial Priesthood" for excluding women from ordination, in addition to
shaky biblical exegesis (or what might be called "isogesis"), these
arguments rest on Thomistic sacramental theology and on "unbroken tradition . . . possessing a normative character."

For Aquinas, a sacrament is constituted by its "res" and its
"sacramentum": the grace of Christ, apart from instrumentality
(res), and the humanly perceptible significance, or sign-value
(sacramentum). Woman is precluded from the sacrament of orders by reason of defect in "natural resemblance," as the Vatican Declaration says. And this is in keeping with a narrow
interpretation of Aquinas, in which no account is taken of cultural limitation or of the defective Aristotelian biology which
informed Aquinas. It is as if the sign-value of woman and therefore the ability of woman to embody the "sacramentum" were
today the same as in the thirteenth century. But as Jeremy
Miller has suggested, "In fact, given the sign-value of feminine
humanity as one might analyze it today, Thomas' theology of orders may indeed provide an argument for ordination of women,
from reasons of fittingness."[12]

As to "unbroken tradition . . . possessing a normative character," this is a powerful argument for all but the most superficial of participants in the debate. What shall we say of such a fundamental change, coming after so many centuries of contrary practice? We must of course note the biblical testimony and early Church practice which, though not determinative, are originative and which point to the prominence of women in the pre-Constantinian Church. But more than this, we must confront the profound truth of the sinfulness of the Church. Triumphalism, about which so much was heard in the early years after the close of Vatican Council II, is by definition the perennial temptation to obscure the differences between the Church on earth and the kingdom of God. And one of the central themes of Christian ethics and ecclesiology deals with the delicate interplay of Church and culture. This theme points to the dialectical relationship which must exist between the two. The Church lives in, and responds in sympathy to, its cultural environment. It proclaims the message of Christ in a manner that can be heard by citizens of the world in each generation and century. Yet, the Church must stand against the evil and complacency of the world, resisting its blandishments. As with slavery, as in the identification of the Church with inhumane social, economic and political forces throughout history, so too in the matter of the rights of women, our Church has been lacking in prophecy. It has simply been wrong! Insight into history and sociology may excuse the Roman Church for mimicking the male chauvinist institutions with which it has shared the spotlight of Western history up till recent times. An honest appraisal of the finiteness of human vision, in other words a knowledge of sin, may also be brought to bear in a sympathetic understanding of the past. But the Church which we love can be exculpated no longer. The day is at hand!

The most profound tool which Roman Catholics have at hand to bring clarity and discernment to our deliberations on the role of women in Church and society is that extraordinary body of social ethics and philosophy that have accrued in modern times from Leo XIII through John Paul II. The "social teachings" are a subtle, sophisticated, rational, yet evangelical, and sustained defense of both the absolute dignity of each human being and the equally imperative claims of the common good. Against collectivizing and dehumanizing social schemes, they insist doggedly that the necessary pre-requisite for a just society is reverence for individuals; against the false autonomy of the liberal democratic ideal of society, they insist on the place of the common good. I shall consider the question of the rights of women as they relate to the common good *of the Church* in a moment. For now, let me offer a few thoughts on the ecclesial rights of women and the rights theory of the Church itself.

David Hollenbach, in a fine recent treatment of the development and characteristics of the Catholic human rights tradition,[13] defines rights in this manner:

> Rights are the conditions for the realization of human worth in action. These human rights concern such diverse human needs as life, food, shelter, sexuality and work. They refer to various domains of freedom and self-determination, such as freedom of expression, association, religion, and communication. They concern different kinds of human inter-relations such as the familial, the economic, the political, the cultural and the religious.[14]

The definition is very much in the spirit of the Catholic social teachings themselves. One can only point to such rights as freedom of expression, religion, and communication and ask what possible meaning these values can possess for women in the Church apart from a change in discipline which does away with their exclusion from the opportunity to participate fully and in all forms of religious expression and communication. It may be argued that the extension of rights rhetoric to include a second order issue such as women's ordination represents an expansionist bias within the dialogue over rights theory, one which dilutes the power and cogency of rights thought and deflects attention from those more primal needs such as life, political participation and economic opportunity which are acknowledged as self-evident rights in humane societies. Yet, the social teachings themselves are characterized, as Hollenbach points out,[15] by an expansionist bias, so that a later document in the evolution of the social teachings, such as John XXIII's *Mater et Magistra,* can identify a whole series of welfare interventions by the state, designed to redress economic imbalances as rights which governments must move to protect. More specifically, Hollenbach has identified an underlying movement in the social teachings from the designation of *personal* rights (such as religious belief) to the extension of these rights to their *social* manifestation (religious expression), culminating in the *instrumental* protection of these personal and social rights (in this example, "full-religious freedom"). The important point is that in this development, most dramatically seen in the social encyclical *Pacem in Terris,*[16] all three levels at which the right is manifest are themselves identified as rights. This marks a new level of political realism for the social teachings and, at least implicitly, acknowledges the conflictual character of human rights theory and advocacy. For identifying the instrumental manifestation of personal and social rights as a human right itself is to lift talk of human rights from the danger of high-blown and vacuous verbalizing. Thus we must demand of the Church what the Church demands of sinful society: the *personal* right of women to be Catholic Christians cannot culminate in a limited *social* expression, however multiple the opportunities for such expression (though even at this level preaching is apparently not one such mode). Women have a right to the full, instrumental manifestation of their personal and social rights both to be Catholic and to express this Catholicity. Without this extension of rights, nothing else but hypocrisy is this powerful magisterial teaching from *Gaudium et Spes:* "With respect to the fundamental rights of the person, every type of discrimination whether based on sex, race, color, social conditions, language or religion is to be eradicated as contrary to God's intent."[17]

And for those who point out that reception of the sacrament of orders is not a right for men or women, let Ruether have the final word:

> This misconstrues the issue. It is not a question of any individual having a right to be ordained as an individ-

ual. It is a matter of an entire group of Christians, over half the membership of the Church, being excluded from the possibility of ordination on the basis of group characteristics such as sex. . . .[18]

Finally, the matter of the achievement of the full rights of women in the Church is a matter as much of the common good as of individual rights. As such it is an issue of social justice; as Hollenbach says, social justice is "the measure which orders personal activities in a way which is suitable for the production of the common good."[19] I have in mind especially the common good of the Church itself. For on the full admission to partnership of women in the Church rests the question of whether the Church will be true to its sublime mission and whether it will strike out boldly against those elements, those " 'manly' activities," in Ruether's phrase, in our society which seek to render the Christian Church innocuous.

Gabriel Moran has argued persuasively that the simplest and most effective way to domesticate the power of an otherwise effective institution is to "identify that institution with women and children."[20] Clearly secularization has led to the subordination of the Church in society. In a startling section of her book, *New Women, New Earth*, Rosemary Radford Ruether has suggested in a dramatic way how this domestication affects male clergy:

> Males in the work world . . . accord the clergy the underhanded contempt with which the masculinist ethic always regards the feminine, that is, that which it has pacified and domesticated in relation to itself. Such men are embarrassed or angered by clergy who "don't know their place" and who try to interfere in things that they "know nothing about," such as political and economic power. Thus the clergy who inherited classical masculinist self-images in relation to women and the congregation now find themselves serving essentially the feminine role in relation to the real power structure of society.[21]

In this domestication of the male clergy and the Church itself lies the foundation of common cause among Catholic men and women. For, "if both the clergy and women must see themselves as victims of this encapsulation [of the Church in the sphere of privatized sentimentality] in the domestic sphere, then they must also recognize each other as common allies in a struggle to overthrow the false schism between 'private morality' and the world of 'real men.' "[22]

It is tragic to view our Church polarized over a question of mutuality and community. These are the very qualities which define the Christian ethos, for:

> . . . the principles of Christian community are founded upon a role transformation between men and women, rulers and ruled. The ministry of the Church is not to be modeled on hierarchies of lordship, but on the *diakonia* of women and servants, while women are freed from exclusive identification with the service role and called to join the circle of disciples and members.[23]

The failure of empathy, the animosity and defensiveness which characterize polemics over the role of women in the Church today is doubly tragic, for it obscures the ultimate value for women and men and for ministry that lies at the heart of the matter. The full integration of women into the life and ministry of the Church is the key to a more effective ministry for all, for it promises a new era of partnership between women and men; a partnership which Letty Russell describes as "a new focus of relationship in which there is continuing commitment and common struggle with a wider community context."[24]

NOTES

1. Lynda M. Glennon, *Women and Dualism*, 1979, p. 17.
2. *Ibid.*, p. 19.
3. Wolfhart Pannenberg, *Theology and the Kingdom of God*, 1969, p. 56.

4. Cf. Alfred North Whitehead, *Religion in the Making*, 1926.

5. Elizabeth Moltmann-Wendel, *Liberty, Equality, Sisterhood*, 1978, p. 67.

6. *Ibid.*, pp. 69f.

7. Alfred North Whitehead, *Adventures of Ideas*.

8. Nancy and Theodore Sizer (eds.), *Moral Education*, 1970, pp. 29–55.

9. Cf. Pope Pius XII, *Summi Pontificatus*.

10. Sacred Congregation for the Doctrine of the Faith, *Origins 6*, February 3, 1977.

11. Rosemary Radford Ruether, *New Women, New Earth*, 1975, p. 4.

12. Jeremy Miller, O.P., "A Note on Aquinas and the Ordination of Women," *New Blackfriars*, Vol. 61, No. 719, 1980, p. 190.

13. David Hollenbach, *Claims in Conflict*, 1979.

14. *Ibid.*, p. 91.

15. *Ibid.*, Chapter 1.

16. *Ibid.*, p. 198.

17. Vatican II, *Declaration on the Church in the Modern World*, 1965, n. 29.

18. Ruether, *op. cit.*, p. 79.

19. Hollenbach, *op. cit.*, p. 151.

20. Gabriel Moran, *Religious Body*, 1975, p. 44.

21. Ruether, *op. cit.*, p. 77.

22. *Ibid.*, p. 82.

23. *Ibid.*, p. 70.

24. Letty M. Russell, *The Future of Partnership*, 1979, p. 18.

Strengths and Limitations of Brotherhood

Gabriel Moran

The crisis of the contemporary world is a crisis of authority. Undoubtedly, one could argue that some other category
(e.g., love, peace, justice) describes the fundamental problem facing men and women today. I will argue, however, that authority
is an especially helpful category both in the breadth of its application and in the powerful focus it gives to personal and institutional issues. Perhaps ultimately "all we need is love," but
penultimately in the political, economic, international and—not
least of all—religious life the question of authority urgently con-
fronts us.

Almost everyone acknowledges that there is a problem of
authority. One cannot look at television, ride a subway or listen
to casual comments on the government without being aware of
the problem. The surprising thing is that there is so little analysis of the problem and even little clarity on what the word "authority" means. I would like to offer here my own brief analysis
of the imagery and language of authority with some advertence
to Christian history and to the revolt against Church authority
in modern times.

The Church shares its problem of authority with other institutions in the modern world. The same rhetorical questions
are heard at ecclesiastical gatherings as at meetings of General
Motors or the National Democratic Party: Why do we have
such poor leadership. Why don't people obey the rules? Why

doesn't anything work anymore? Do you remember the good old days?

The last question leads into the most pessimistic interpretation of the Church's authority problem. In this reading, the Church may share the problem with other organizations but it is far worse off. Its glory days are all in the past and it has been on the downhill for a long time. The erosion of its position of authority is evident to everyone's eyes. The enemies of the Church make this assumption, but many Church people, including officials, also seem to admit or at least to suspect the validity of such a pessimistic reading.

This essay offers not so much an optimistic interpretation but a refusal to buy the assumption on which pessimism is based. The Church does share the problem of authority with the modern world, and so it cannot simply serve up an answer to the problem. Nonetheless, the age and the funded experience of the Church can be read as advantages. But what the Church has to offer will be heard only if one challenges *both* the common ancient meaning of authority and the common modern meaning. I will presently spell out how we today move between two hopes for establishing authority and how both hopes have proved groundless.

I would like to make one prefatory comment about rebellion and rebels. Anyone who has ever taught a class, chaired a meeting, run an organization or presided over a government has had to confront the rebel. When you are the one who is "in charge" you are probably not an enthusiast of rebellion; yet in another setting on another day the roles might be reversed. When rebellion is not directed at us, most of us would admit that rebellion can be a good thing or at least that it holds promising possibilities. We would probably wish to contrast rebellion to, for example, revolution and set criteria for distinguishing one from the other. Albert Camus, in his well-known study *The Rebel*, emphasizes that rebellion accepts limits while revolution does not.

A similar distinction that defines rebellion is offered by Elie Wiesel in describing the Hasidic leader Levi-Yitzak. Wiesel has described Levi-Yitzak as ranting and raging in public outbursts, directing his rebellion even at God. But, says Wiesel, "it all depends on where the rebel chooses to stand. From inside his community, he may say everything. Let him step outside it, and he will be denied this right. The revolt of the believer is not that of the renegade; the two do not speak in the name of the same anguish."[1]

Wiesel and Camus would agree that a chief characteristic distinguishing rebel from renegade, rebel from revolutionary, is the ideal of brotherhood. "Jewish tradition allows a man to say anything to God provided it be on behalf of man."[2] The first-century Church and the eighteenth-century enlightenment would agree with this twentieth-century ideal of fraternity or brotherhood. When the choice is between the repression of authoritarian regimes and the solidarity of fraternal community, no one—including myself—is going to bad-mouth brotherhood. Nevertheless, while brotherhood has been a sustained and sustaining ideal for Christianity, Judaism, Islam, and secular humanism, the limitations of the ideal have seldom been noted. The fact that brotherhood leaves out at least fifty percent of the human race is no small flaw when one is talking about hopes, ideals and contexts for activity. Furthermore, if that ideal has been too narrowly conceived for human beings it is too narrow even for men and has distorted past rebellions.

What I suggest is that a new kind of rebelling is upon us today and no one is very clear about its form. It is not Kierkegaard's lonely man of faith, nor Nietzsche's superman, nor Sartre's existential man; it is a rebellion in which women and feminine imagery play a central role. For the first time in Western history the very ideal of brotherhood is vulnerable to severe criticism. Brotherhood conceived as a union to overthrow fatherhood is today insufficient as an idealized vision of society.

More than a decade ago I began saying that the two most important religious movements in the country are feminism and ecology. The two movements might in fact be parts of a single movement. They are central to religion today because they concern the power that governs human life and cosmic reality. What we have today is a rebellion of the earth against its dominating species. The conflict of "man and nature" has been building up for centuries but it is headed for some new arrangement in the century to come. Between the man who set out to rule the earth and the creatures who will no longer bear his arrogance there is womankind who has a foot in both camps.

In making reference to this global and cosmic issue I have not lost sight of the mundane question of running organizations. The technocratic mentality of modern times thinks of authority as an administrative problem or a lack of information. A strength of the Church is that it has a sense that authority involves a struggle of angels and archangels, principalities and powers. Feminism and ecology represent a return to grappling with ultimate issues of power. Of course, not everyone who cries feminism or ecology is speaking of the kingdom of God. Nonetheless, the crisis of authority today cannot be met without admitting into the discussion the issues of feminism and ecology. Despite their sometimes seeming to be opposed to current Church forms of authority, feminism and ecology are two of the sources of a new form of authority that can be true to the Church's past and workable for today.

What then is authority and why is it in crisis? To set up a response I would like to refer to one book in particular: Richard Sennett's *Authority*.[3] Despite a mixed review from critics the book deserves to be called an interesting and admirable attempt to grapple with the problem. Sennett uses a diversity of methods ranging from historical narrative through fiction to sociology. His material reveals the inadequacy of the two main forms of authority in modern Western culture. What is most disappointing is the answer he proposes because it is patently inadequate to the crisis he has described.

Although Sennett's history and fiction clearly delineate the problem of authority his own definition of the word "authority" remains fuzzy. When a problem is as great as authority is, one cannot simply declare: "The real meaning of authority is. . . ." Nevertheless, I think one must, while acknowledging the ambiguities of meaning and the fact that one's own stipulated meaning will not find universal acceptance, write with consistency and in a way that illuminates the available data. Starting with the book's introduction, Sennett does not seem to do that. He writes: "Authority, fraternity, solitude and ritual are four distinctively social emotions. Three of them build bonds to other people."[4] The next paragraph on the same page says: "Authority is a bond between people who are unequal."[5] At another place where the author directly addresses the meaning of the word, he writes: "Authority, however, is still inherently an act of imagination. It is not a thing; it is a search for solidity and security in the strength of others which will seem to be like a thing."[6] Is authority an emotion, a bond, an act of imagination, or a search? Perhaps all of these meanings are somehow relevant, but Sennett leaves these and other meanings scattered through his text without a consistent relation.

I do not think that a consistent and comprehensive meaning of the word "authority" should be that difficult to come by. From Sennett's own material as well as other writers whom I will refer to, I would claim that the question of authority is the question of the legitimate exercise of power. The word does shade off into other meanings, but there is a clear enough issue being raised today when people speak of a crisis of authority: How is an organization credible when it tries to impose order? How do large institutions justify their use of power in a world court of opinion? What gives an institution or someone "representing" the institution the right to issue orders to people who are expected to comply? Authority, most simply, is the legitimation of power.

In proposing this definition of authority, I am able to include imagining, feeling, bonding, and search. However, it is misleading to equate authority to any of these elements or all of them. More important, I am closely relating power and authority but also clearly distinguishing them. Power is an unavoidable fact that goes beyond the human world. Authority, in contrast, is a particular arrangement of power that can be undermined and destroyed. It includes the human perception of what is right and proper.

I said above that there is a common ancient form of authority and a common modern form and that both are failing us today. In the ancient form authority is based upon origins or foundation, that is, one should obey because the world has been so established from the beginning. To the question "Why should I?" the answer was: "Because the gods (or the founders) determined that you should. That is the way things always have been and always will be." In Western culture this form of authority fused with a patriarchal form so that the two often appear to be the same. Within the biological family the father was in charge, and for the nation or the universe there were fathers or quasi-fathers who had issued orders.

Most authors, including Sennett, equate the traditional form of authority to patriarchy, but that is to miss the full force of traditional authority. An individual father or father figure could claim authority because he stood in the place of some greater figure who had set up the present order of things. A continuity of tradition was therefore crucial to this form of authority, a fact that is obscured if one simply refers to patriarchy. In Western history this aspect of the authority issue takes palpable form with the myth of origins in Roman civilization and the apostolic era of the Christian Church. Authority is exercised and made present by legally established rulers who stand in physical continuity with the founders of the institution.

Modernity is the attempt to overthrow the traditional form of authority. The modern West is an experiment that began by attacking the traditional form. However, as I have indicated, there was some ambiguity in that form. Was the problem the myth of the founders, the image of continuity, or the representative father figures? Different parts of the modern world picked out one or more elements in that picture to attack. What emerged from all the attacks was a quest for autonomy that was correlated with an assumption of reasonableness. To the question "Why should I?" the answer was: "Because it is the reasonable thing to do." The usually veiled corollary to this answer was: "And if you do not see some things as reasonable that you should see are reasonable, then society will have to compel you to be reasonable."

Sennett is one of many writers today who say that the quest for autonomy is not working and cannot work.[7] The hope that everyone would eventually become reasonable (through mass education, the spread of democracy, the increase of wealth) has proved illusory in the twentieth century. The eighteenth-century *philosophes* and the nineteenth-century founders of Marxism were sure they were ridding the world of the superstitions and magical presences that oppressed mankind. If the entire social order could be obliterated, then each man could start without a burden and obedience would be to sweet reasonableness. "Everything that exists around us," said Saint-Just, "must change and come to an end because everything around us is unjust. . . . Man drops his anchor in the future and presses to his heart the posterity which bears no blame for the evils of the present."[8] The traditional form of authority is here identified with the past as a whole, while the patriarchal image in that past does not receive the specific attention it should have. In John Locke's *Second Treatise on Government* there is a simple split between the family and all other organization; in the family the father would rule and elsewhere autonomy would be the rule. But patriarchy has deep roots in biology and in the psyche. When autonomy fails, then patriarchy resurfaces. Locke, Saint-Just and Marx could not have imagined that in the twentieth century Josef Stalin would be saying: "The state is a family and I am your father."[9]

Stalin is one of many deadly portents that authority as personal autonomy is an illusion. Life was never wholly reasonable in the past and we are not getting closer to such a world today. The quest for autonomy has involved an attempt to avoid the questions of authority. What is going to hold together people in workable groups and organizations? Who is going to decide what institutions, larger and more powerful than ever, are going to do?

Sennett's answer to the dilemma of patriarchy and autonomy is shockingly inadequate. It amounts to techniques for "disrupting the chain of command." While this approach might, for example, improve conditions in a factory, the underlying and profound question of the nature of authority is left untouched. Furthermore, simply encouraging people to violate codes of conduct could further erode a respect for authority. One of the most interesting comments on Sennett's proposal was made by the Marxist historian Eugene Genovese: "The Catholic Church, immeasurably wiser than a thousand years of sneering critics, has always demanded respect for the office regardless of the sins and frailties of the officeholders. . . . It is the priesthood not the priest that demands respect and obedience. Since Professor Sennett supports authority in principle, his failure to confront this gnawing problem leaves his proposals for disruption open to challenges and doubts."[10]

Genovese's important distinction here is sadly neglected today. It is closely related to the ambiguity I pointed to earlier in what constituted the traditional form of authority. The Catholic Church's authority was not paternalistic in a narrow and immediate sense. Every "father," including the Pope, claimed only to represent the authority of the founding era of the Church. The theological doctrine of the efficacy of the sacraments clearly enunciated the distinction. Unfortunately in practice the Catholic Church seemed to many people to be an institution in which the clerical class claimed authority for itself. The Protestant Reformation rebelled against that development by appealing directly to the written texts of the founding age. However, texts are never a full answer to the question of authority. The texts can be a part of an authoritarian system or (when people are literate) they can be part of the image of authority as a search for autonomy. The Reformation gave the Church access to the modern world; it also gave the Church a share in the modern world's problem with authority.

If the two available images of authority are inadequate, where can we turn for help? The answer, I would argue, lies deeper within those two inadequate images of patriarchy and autonomy. There must be some truth to both of them even if neither is able to satisfy the needs of contemporary institutions. Here is where Christian history may be able to teach some lesson to the contemporary world even while the Church in turn learns from the political and social experiments of modernity.

There is a truth to the traditional form of authority that Western culture has rejected to its own peril. The father who has given us life has an obvious right to exercise some control over his progeny. The fathers of the Church or the fathers of the U.S. Constitution also have some right to guide their descendants within the boundaries of their respective organizations.

But two things are missing in most discussions of this form of authority. Why is the mother figure who is an equal source of life not also recognized as a guide? What is the significance of the generations between the founding age and the present? I think that these two questions are connected. The power that history gives over to the father stands outside and above history, not the power of the first age but the power before the first age. If the mother as well as the father gives birth, then the authority of the founders would be supplemented and developed by each succeeding generation. The phrase "if the mother ... gives birth" may seem to be a peculiar and unnecessary phrase, but that fact is precisely what has been denied throughout most of recorded history. The woman was seen as a receptacle for the father's generation of sons and (by imperfection) daughters. Authority was not maternal because women supposedly had little to do with the generating of children.

Since denying a generative role to women runs counter to obvious sense experience, there must have been a powerful reason for obscuring the fact. In the Western philosophic tradition and the Hebrew-Christian religious tradition, the woman was seen as a defective man and therefore in need of governing. The men had authority, the women and children obeyed. The picture did not change until well into the modern period when medical and biological facts could no longer be denied. Galen in the second century had a more advanced knowledge of woman's role in procreation than did physicians in the fourteenth century. The reason for this ignorance slips out in a comment of a sixteenth-century physician: "Woman is a most arrogant and extremely intractable animal, and she would be worse if she came to realize that she is no less perfect and no less fit to wear breeches than man. To check woman's continual desire to dominate, nature arranged things so that every time she thinks of her supposed lack she may be humbled and shamed."[11]

Is this fear of "woman's continual desire to dominate" a fantasy without foundation? The answer of a number of writers today, including some feminists, is: No. Given our methods of child rearing, nearly all men first experience authority as maternal. For the infant the great power in the world is the mother;

she has an unbounded right, in the child's view, to dispense food, warmth, security, and life itself. It is a power that envelops, and the child must soon seek refuge. "To mother-raised humans, male authority is bound to look like a reasonable refuge from female authority. We come eventually, of course, to resist male authority too."[12] The same writer goes on to say that both Freud and Fromm missed the point in talking about the flight to authoritarianism because of a fear of freedom. "We rush into the trap of male tyranny not to escape freedom but more total tyranny: female."[13]

Whether there was a full-fledged matriarchy before the historical period is a matter for speculation. But the issue of child rearing is open to immediate examination. A different angle on patriarchy has been opened by those who have seen the question through child rearing in a post-Freudian age. Early infancy does powerfully affect our imagery throughout life. "Most men spend their lives trying to palliate those unconscious, archaic fears by rendering women powerless in the world of daily experience."[14] Rituals of subjugation temporarily allay the fears but the fears remain. Two conclusions follow: (1) we are all, women as well as men, affected by a fear of maternal authority even as we continually complain about patriarchy; (2) we have a way out of the fruitless conflict of patriarchy and autonomy, that is, we have a concrete and urgent change needed in our method of child rearing.

The argument here is not the standard game of blaming the mother for whatever goes wrong. The mother in caring for the child is doing what she should. The presence of other adults, preferably but not necessarily including the father, as early as possible in infancy would change our experience of power and authority. From the very beginning the "quest for autonomy" would be situated as a search to participate in a mutuality of power.

All of us in the modern Western world are in quest of personal autonomy. We are also desirous that life be as reasonable as possible. Having fled the maternal we put our trust in patriarchy until we outgrow that too. Personal autonomy for women as well as men today gets pitted against the father figure. But the obstacle to "liberation" in the U.S. family has never been the father. On the contrary, we need to encourage the social role of fathering[15] and we need the strength associated with father figures. We also need a sense of motherhood integral to the family and a sense of nurturing that has been associated with mother figures. In short, we need to experience authority as our response to interdependence and our response to maternal, paternal, sisterly and brotherly aspects of the past within our present.

What conclusions can be drawn with reference to Church authority? What can the Church teach the modern world and in turn learn from studies of interdependence today?

1. The "authority of the Church" should never be equated with the current form of Church administration. Conservatives as much as liberals should agree to this principle. The Church has grown throughout the centuries, entering into exchange with the surrounding culture. With the break of Eastern and Western churches and then with the Protestant Reformation the whole Church incorporated a variety of administrative styles. Authority is manifested in a mixture of patriarchy and autonomy. But as I have indicated it would be unwise to identify either of these current forms with the form that the Church must have. While Protestant groups that had stressed autonomy are today looking for discipline, ritual and cohesion, the Roman Catholic Church that had appeared so paternal (or papal) has been incorporating the search for personal autonomy.

It would be tragic if such evolution were conceived merely as a defensive retreat toward some middle ground. Paternalism and autonomy are not lesser and greater amounts of the same thing. Both are profound but partial truths; both must be retained in an image more appropriate for the future. Paternalism in the Church is a distortion of the demand that authority be based on the whole of experience. Paternalism seemed to past generations the way to include the family, our ancestors and the non-human elements of the universe. As we give up the identification of authority and paternalism (in churches that stress tradition) we have to be sure of getting richer imagery.

Something similar must be said of the image of autonomy. We have to give up on a meaning of autonomy as an individual without ties or opposition while at the same time insisting on a "relative autonomy" or a distinctiveness that comes through relationships. We should decide for ourselves but never on our own authority. The Christian movement from within Judaism set out to make men free, to carry forward with the Pharisaic movement the sense of the individual's autonomy or uniqueness, symbolized especially in the doctrine of personal resurrection. The last barrier to autonomy, individual death, was to be transcended. Here was the greatness of the Church and the source of endless troubles for Church authority, with the Protestant Reformation a chief case in point. Herbert Butterfield writes: "Precisely because the medieval Church did its work so well, it was bound to promote a kind of world that would be liable to rebel against its authority."[16] As I indicated in my prefatory comment, rebellion within Judaism or Christianity is not necessarily a sign of institutional failure or personal disloyalty. Rebellion is perhaps what should be expected of religious traditions that teach people to be free.

2. We should always distinguish between the office of authority and the person who holds the office. That means never saying "Church authority" when one is referring to the man who exercises an office of Church authority. The distinction is an important one both for those who occupy such offices and for those who are critical of people in office. If a man is not doing the job as well as he could, he should be criticized no matter how high the office. If a man proves incapable of doing the job there should be a way of removing him. The modern world has rules of political discourse and procedures of judicial review for handling these matters. In some ways the Church is under-institutionalized, forgetting its own distinction of the personal and official.

In carrying out his office, a man (or woman) has a wide range of styles available from past Church history. Without doing violence to an historic office he might contribute to a reshaping of the design of Church offices. Some ecclesiastical officials seem to think that the only image in Church history is a shepherd leading sheep. Without disparaging the beautiful parable of Jesus, I would still judge that the metaphor of leading sheep is an extremely limited one for today's population. St. Paul's image of the "body of Christ" is one that is as relevant to the twentieth century as to the first. Paul used the image in conflicting ways, sometimes making Christ the head and sometimes the whole body. In either case his image moves us away from the identification of Church office with either pre-modern patriarchy or modern bureaucracy. The Church can be conceived as an organic interplay of many peoples and offices. To comply with authority then means to respond appropriately to the needs of the whole body.

3. The history of the Church is marked by a series of communal movements that attempted to embody the meaning of authority as a sharing in the power of the whole Church. Most of these movements went down heretical paths or they were absorbed into the existing form of the Church. I think it is still too early in the history of the Church to declare all such movements unwise and unworkable. We could learn why movements in the past failed and how we might use the resources of the twentieth century to better the chances of new movements.

The first centuries of the Christian era spawned several groups that ended in Gnosticism, a movement that has lately attracted scholarly attention.[17] The Gnostic groups can sound attractive, especially their insistence upon sexual equality. Before assuming that the whole Church should have gone that route it is advisable to note that sex was not to be divisive because sex was to be eliminated. A premature arrival at the end of time makes sex, institutions, and all forms of authority unnecessary. The one problem such groups have is how to convince everyone that time is at an end.

The monastic movement after St. Benedict represents one of the more successful communal movements in the history of Christianity. In searching for a greater authority the monks protested against the limitations of all institutions, including the current form of the Church. A familiar counsel warned every monk to avoid associating with women and bishops.[18] The eventual ordination of most monks indicates that they were more successful in avoiding the former than the latter. A paternal form of Church thus absorbed the potential contribution of fraternal authority. Yet to this day writers turn to the ideal of brotherhood: "The most promising aspect I see before us is a sort of free-wheeling, post-industrial monasticism—communitarian forms that delicately combine the need for personal growth with an economy of simple means and fulfilling work."[19]

The fourteenth-century reform movements like the very early Church issued in groups whose orthodoxy was suspect.[20] At the extreme were the "Brothers and Sisters of the Free Spirit" who ended by saying that "God is self" and "self is God." Hierarchical forms of authority were to disappear along with sexual discrimination. So also would there be an end to codes of ethical responsibility. A more orthodox group that said some similar things was the "Friends of God." They saw clergy and laity on an equal footing and supported women as Church leaders. They too spoke of the Godhead beyond God and the divinization of man by Christ. As was typical of the mystical tradition they rejected a religion of fear and reward.

The Friends of God and other forms of practical piety in the late Middle Ages formed the background for the Reformation. Luther and Calvin took over the discipline, piety and communal experience of monasticism even as they attacked the monasteries of their time. The Reformation placed "the saints" out in the world with discipline and piety located in the family. Protestantism has largely succeeded in its emphasis upon individual and family. But communal movements, that is, intimate groups larger than the family, remain a pressing need in the twentieth century.

4. I would finally suggest that feminism, along with ecology, may provide a missing key to past communal movements. Women were important to the beginning of monasticism but they were quickly excluded. When many of the most learned women of the Middle Ages went to the convent it was an experience of daughterhood rather than sisterhood. Women played a major role in a great many of the heretical movements. Friedrich Heer writes of the twelfth century: "Women were tired of the masculine ascendency: they disliked being chattels in the marriage market and the objects of monkish suspicion and con-

tempt. Looking for a way to escape from this oppression they found it in education, of the mind and of the spirit. Courtly culture and Catharism both flourished under the protection of noble ladies."[21]

The contemporary feminist movement has echoes in almost every century of Church history. It would be tragic if we learn nothing from past experience. Women are saying more clearly than ever that patriarchy and autonomy do not work, that brotherhood is a preferable idea but still inadequate. Women hold the key to building an authority pattern on the interdependence of all things created and all things in God. A form of authority in which each woman and man responds to the body as a whole would be a stronger power and yet a more freeing power. The time is not ripe for pessimism if the Church will only discover the breadth of its own past and listen to the loyal rebellion of the present.

NOTES

1. Elie Wiesel, *Souls on Fire* (New York, Random House, 1972), p. 111.

2. *Ibid.*

3. Richard Sennett, *Authority* (New York, Knopf, 1980).

4. *Ibid.*, p. 10.

5. *Ibid.*

6. *Ibid.*, p. 197.

7. An important background to the question is Max Horkheimer, *Eclipse of Reason* (New York, Seabury, 1974).

8. See Sennett, *op. cit.*, p. 134.

9. *Ibid.*, p. 75.

10. Eugene Genovese, "Review of 'Authority,'" *New York Times Book Review,* July 13, 1980.

11. See Frances Gies and Joseph Gies, *Women in the Middle Ages* (New York, Harper, 1980), p. 51.

12. Dorothy Dinnerstein, *The Mermaid and the Minotaur* (New York, Harper and Row, 1976), p. 175.

13. *Ibid.*, p. 187.

14. Lillian Rubin, *Women of a Certain Age* (New York, Harper and Row, 1979), p. 71.

15. A new literature on fatherhood has grown up in the last decade; see, for examples, Henry Biller and Dennis Meredith, *Father Power* (New York, Anchor, 1975); Eliot Daley, *Father Feelings* (New York, Morrow, 1978).

16. Herbert Butterfield, *Christianity and History* (New York, Scribner, 1950), p. 35.

17. See Elaine Pagels, *The Gnostic Gospel* (New York, 1980); Raymond Brown, *The Community of the Beloved Disciple* (New York, Paulist, 1979).

18. William Clebsch, *Christianity in European History* (New York, Oxford, 1979), pp. 67f.

19. Theodore Roszak, *Person/Planet* (New York, Anchor, 1978), p. 301.

20. See Bengt Hoffman's "Introduction" to *The Theologia Germanica of Martin Luther* (New York, Paulist, 1980).

21. Friedrich Heer, *The Medieval World: Europe 1100–1350* (Cleveland, World, 1961), p. 163.

THE EXPERIENCE OF
WOMEN

Is Partnership Possible? Ordained Men and Unordained Women in Ministry

Gloria Durka

Most of us who work in Church-related settings have witnessed a conversation between a man in a position of authority in the Church and a woman who wants to participate in the work of the Church. It usually goes something like this. He asks, "Just what do you women really want? Aren't you already taking an active part in the liturgy? More and more of you are members of pastoral teams, parish councils, and even diocesan councils. You are involved in all sorts of social services; you run retreat houses and hospitals. Some of you hold positions that used to be reserved for men." To which she replies: "Yes, but we are not involved in pastoral work on the level at which strategic decisions are made. While some of us have been appointed to all sorts of posts, we do not really feel responsible."

The conversation usually ends in mutual misunderstanding.

What *do* women want? Simply put, they want more *influence* and *responsibility*. They want what a recent document directs priests to affirm, i.e., shared ministry:

> It is essential for the life and service of the Church that priests encourage women in responding to the call to assume more influential and responsible positions of leadership and service in the Church and in society.

> Priests have a serious responsibility to help ensure that decision-making processes at parish, diocesan and national levels incorporate the voices and the insights of women.[1]

This directive can only be taken seriously if ordained men and unordained women are able to transcend the cultural barriers that polarize their individual visions of ministry. Two of these barriers are *clericalism* and *sexism*. These two "isms" work against the vision of the Church presented by the documents of the Second Vatican Council.

The documents of the Council call every segment of Church to a priestly life, a life of love, and a life of service. This vision of the Church has profoundly altered present-day understanding of Christian ministry. Baptism is seen as the basic validation one needs to assume the role of Christian minister. Service to the people of God on behalf of the Church is no longer viewed as the single task of the ordained clergy. The documents state clearly that the ordained and the unordained have their own responsibility for the mission of the Church, and even though that responsibility takes many forms, all ecclesial ministry is one.

Clericalism: Its Effects on Women

The concept of shared ministry envisioned by the Second Vatican Council is a reversal of the hierarchical model of priestly ministry espoused by the Church in the past. This shift in ecclesiology can be the source of tension for ordained ministers if they have not been theologically or practically prepared for it. Many priests were prepared for a priesthood that consolidated all the functions of ministry in themselves as priests. They had the sole responsibility for the spiritual life of the laity, and they were often charged with the physical and financial maintenance of large corporate structures for which they had little or no training.

Because achievement is so tied to his image of manhood, the

ordained minister often feels he must function as the sole initiator, planner, and decision-maker in his parish or other work site. Such a perception also derives from the kind of seminary training that created an unreal world for the ordination candidate, a world in which he was set apart and idealized. After ordination, such men can experience tension because of the awesome expectations that they themselves, or others, place on them. Many consider the sharing of pastoral functions with unordained women to be a real diminishment of their own priesthood. If an ordained male can only identify and value himself as a person through the tasks he performs, it may be extremely difficult for him to share those functions with an unordained woman.[2]

Until quite recently, seminarians were taught to avoid interaction with women and to fear its possible consequences. Now, the Church is encouraging dialogue, shared ministry, and acceptance of women in new ministries and positions of authority. It is only natural, then, that many men who were trained to avoid women are now threatened and fearful of the consequences to their own role of authority and service which would result from women assuming broadened ministerial functions.

Bernard Cooke suggests that the development of the clergy-laity division over the centuries, together with the control of ministries by the hierarchy, has impoverished the Church and left the laity in a position of passivity and powerlessness. Their ministerial gifts for the most part remained dormant and under-developed.[3] For women, this situation has been particularly debilitating. Because they are women, they are barred from any public, official function in the proclamation of the good news which has been the sole prerogative of the male, celibate clerics. The holders of all ecclesiastical offices (diaconate, presbyterate, and episcopate) are exclusively men; leadership and pastoral oversight are closely bound up with those offices, and the various functions connected with them (teaching, legislation and administration) are consequently exercised only by men; women have no share in them (this finds legal expression in CIC 968, 1). Women can only be involved in pastoral and catechetical work in a very limited way—if at all—in certain restricted areas of the Church's life. Theological teaching and research are still largely the domain of men (although feminine theologians are now challenging this exclusivity). The way in which the idea of God is expressed corresponds to the actual power structure: he is male (Father, Lord). Ecclesiastical language, as well as visual representations, confirms and sanctions male predominance in the Church.[4]

The Church in its attitude and practice has limited the role of women to nurturance and left greater freedom and power to men. Most of the struggle for women's liberation in the Church centers now on questioning the clericalism and sexism that have oppressed women. So far our discussion in this essay has centered around *clericalism*, i.e., "the bias that attributes only to the ordained ministers the rights, privileges, abilities and responsibilities which belong to all baptized Christians."[5] While some changes have occurred in the last decade with an ever so gradual increase in the number of women who hold parish and diocesan leadership positions, discrimination is the result of sex role stereotyping. It is known as *sexism*, and it deserves honest scrutiny here.

Sexism: Its Effects on Women

Sex role stereotyping permeates our culture and affects not only the way men perceive women, but the way women perceive themselves. This perception in turn colors a man's expectations regarding female behavior and a woman's expectations of herself. We have only to look to our popular culture to see the forms it takes. The Broadway musical *My Fair Lady*, just for one example, tells it all. "Women are irrational, that's all there is to that. Their heads are full of cotton, hay and rags," sings Henry Higgins, Edwardian gentleman, agitated hero, and manager of the beautiful Eliza's career. He goes on to describe Eliza, and all women in general, as "exasperating, irritating, vacillating, calculating, agitating, maddening, and infuriating hags," and to query:

Why is thinking something women never do?
Why is logic never even tried;

Straightening out their hair is all they ever do,
Why don't they straighten up the mess inside?

These lyrics, written in the 1950's, include the most popular stereotypes about women prevalent in our society today. Women
are, in short, oversensitive, empty-headed, and unable to make
up their minds in a rational fashion about anything that counts.
Today's men are little different from their Edwardian grandfa-
thers. Many ask themselves the same question which Higgins
did: "Why can't a woman be more like a man?" However,
should a woman attempt that less than desirable metamorphosis
by adopting "male" behavior, she becomes a "calculating, agitating, infuriating hag." This is the dilemma which today's unordained woman faces: in order to succeed in ministerial
leadership positions she must behave in a manner commonly
designated as male. Such behavior assures her loss of femininity
and often reaps sarcastic epithets such as "pushy" or "domineer-
ing." The resultant Catch-22 keeps a woman immobilized and
locked in low-level positions: if she is deferential and feminine,
she won't be taken seriously; if she is assertive and independent,
she not only won't succeed but risks losing her identity as a
woman.

Stereotypic evaluations of behavior, such as those of Henry
Higgins, serve several functions simultaneously:

• With a few words Higgins expresses a commonly held
notion believed to be so obvious that it requires no proof or explanation. By relying on a stereotype, men avoid using an objective yardstick to measure a woman's behavior. If they have a
convenient supply of stock phrases on hand which are equally
accepted by all other men, they can easily handle any situation
simply by labeling the woman in question.

• Stereotypes foster polarization of the sexes. Women are
one way (agitating, vacillating, illogical) and men another (firm,
decisive, rational). Such thinking encourages men to join ranks
and work as a group to keep women out of the mainstream of
power. Male and female colleagues become "them" and "us,"
two disparate groups divided by sex instead of united by common goals.

- Stereotypes also justify maintaining the status quo: women are unreliable; consequently, they don't belong in critical, responsible positions.
- Stereotypes allow men to avoid facing their role in job discrimination. A man in a leadership position may challenge and goad his female colleague or employee until she reacts emotionally. His interpretation of her behavior will rely on stereotypes: women are emotional and oversensitive; this staff member is a woman, therefore she isn't tough enough to handle the job. This explanation of female behavior excuses men from any responsibility in such situations, and justifies the belief that women don't belong in important positions because they don't hold up well under pressure.
- The use of a handy label allows men to avoid confronting their own anxieties and insecurities about competing with women.
- Labeling also permits work evaluation to be based on subjective, imprecise criteria instead of by objective standards.[6]

While such stereotyping is injurious to both sexes, it is especially debilitating for women. Several important research studies seem to bear this out. For example, according to one study, women experience anxiety when confronted with the possibility of success because the competence, independence, and competition prerequisite to such success are inconsistent with our culture's stereotypic view of women.[7] Women expect negative, not positive, consequences from high achievement and thus avoid success in order to escape social rejection. Should a woman believe that being in a leadership position is contrary to her definition of womanhood, she may reject such a position rather than experience a basic threat to her femininity.

If women fear success because of an implied loss of femininity, what does this say about our culture's definition of what it means to be feminine? In our society, the feminine ideal is still sweet, pretty, and polite. Translated into practical terms, this means submissive, deferential and dependent on her looks to get ahead. Above all, she is never smarter than the nearest male. What does measuring up to such an ideal imply for an unordained woman working in Church-related positions? Women who conform to this standard, even unconsciously, can sabotage their jobs but remain true to their culture's feminine ideal, or they can adopt so-called male characteristics. Because our society defines assertive behavior as desirable in a man and undesirable in a woman, women who are highly motivated, independent, and achievement oriented are not viewed as possible leaders but as potential troublemakers, whereas the opposite is true for a man.

When carried one step further, this model of a successful leader (aggressive, independent, virile, rational) becomes a model for the healthy male in general. According to a study done by the Brovermans and their colleagues, mental health practitioners themselves hold a double standard of mental health.[8] When asked to produce a model of a healthy, mature female and compare it to one of a healthy, mature male, all the participants in the study, including male and female psychologists and social workers, described the healthy woman as more submissive, less independent, less analytical, and more excitable than the healthy male. Thus a woman who attempts to develop the necessary characteristics to successfully function in her job is labeled a troublemaker by her employer, "masculine" by her colleagues, and abnormal by health professionals. It is no wonder that women either withdraw from applying for leadership positions, or deflect their energy into positions where their "traditional" talents as women are fostered and approved.

There are several other ways that sex role stereotypes affect women who work in Church-related jobs:

• Sex role stereotypes keep women from being seen as they are as opposed to what someone expects them to be. So, if a pastor believes that femininity is synonymous with deference and tact, his belief will affect how he appraises the performance of the woman who works as the director of religious education, for example. If she is straightforward and assertive, both positive qualities for a person in such a position, he will react to her as masculine and aggressive, failing to see her for the dynamic, strong person and good DRE that she is.

• Sex role stereotypes keep people from interpreting experience in a new way as opposed to pre-conceived terms. In the above example the pastor is unable to perceive the DRE in any new way, e.g., as an integrated, whole person instead of a "masculine" (and therefore unacceptable) woman.

• Sex role stereotypes justify negative responses to any female behavior that is contrary to one's expectation.

• Sex role stereotypes exert strong pressure on women to act in a traditional way. For example, a woman who receives unpleasant reactions to a certain behavior (such as assertiveness or straightforwardness) may revert to the typical "feminine" behavior that brings praise, rewards, and no credibility. Thus sex role stereotypes are a strong conservative force and maintain the status quo.

• Sex role stereotypes encourage people to react to women in terms of role, not professional, expectations. In a job interview, a young woman with an M.A. in religious education may be asked, "Are you married?" or "When do you plan to have children?" or "Does your husband have a permanent job here?" instead of questions about her professional aspirations and plans. Although such questions are illegal, they still occur throughout the job market, and churches and Sunday schools are no exception. If a woman refuses to answer them, she may be labeled angry and defensive (emotional, just like a woman). If she does reply, she is cooperating with the stereotypic role expectations which serve to keep her from breaking out of this mold.

• Sex role stereotypes keep us from developing an objective and independent yardstick by which to measure professional behavior, be it male or female. The statements "Women are . . ." or "Men are . . ." keep us from saying "People are . . ."

Through the Looking Glass: Confronting Our Own Stereotypes

What can we do to change this situation and to resist sex role stereotypes? First and most important, we must bring them out into the open and recognize the extent to which they permeate our *thinking* and affect our *behavior*.

Given below is an exercise designed to help define one's concept of femininity. Ask yourself: "How do I define femininity?"

By actions?	YES	NO
By looks?	YES	NO
By language and expression?	YES	NO
By personal style?	YES	NO
By occupation?	YES	NO
By anything else? (If yes, by what?)	YES	NO

What does this exercise tell you about your *conceptual* framework?

These two lists identify the characteristics and actions most commonly associated with women and men.[9] Do you recognize any of your own attitudes in these stereotypic categories?

A. Women	B. Men
Sensitive	Ambitious
Emotional	Aggressive
Loyal	Independent
Gentle	Blunt
Passive	Dominant
Dependent	Adventurous
Submissive	Unconcerned with emotions (his own and others)
Manipulative	Straightforward
Compassionate	Decisive
Talkative	Data-oriented
Tactful	Direct
Indecisive	Logical and objective
Excitable	Worldly
Retiring	Ambitious
People-oriented	Self-confident
Security-oriented	Competitive and active
Seductress	Achievement-oriented

.1. Women	B. Men
Tolerant and kind	Strong professional orientation
Yielding	Strong goal orientation
Cooperative	Tough-minded
Nurturing	Analytical
Creative and artistic	
Tender	Practical
Intuitive	Consistent
Concerned with appearance	
Reactive	
Self-effacing	

Can you add any characteristics to these lists? What do these lists tell you about yourself?

Our *behavior* often reflects our pre-suppositions. Following is a chart designed to help the ordained male look at some of his behavior toward unordained women, and to suggest an alternative to any stereotypic behavior that is recognized in the given situation.

SOME TYPICAL GAMES MEN PLAY

GAME	MESSAGE	ALTERNATIVE
Expect the woman to take notes at meetings.	She's a subordinate.	Request that notes be taken on a rotating basis.
Request that she get (and/or prepare) coffee.	She's a caretaker.	Suggest that this task be performed on a rotating basis.
Bypass her input at a meeting.	Women are inferior. They don't know as much as men do.	Acknowledge all input; assign space for input on the agenda.

SOME TYPICAL GAMES MEN PLAY

GAME	MESSAGE	ALTERNATIVE
Discount her observation.	Women aren't rational thinkers.	Focus attention on the points being made.
Call her "dear" or "honey."	Women are inferior, childlike. Don't take them seriously.	Avoid such expressions entirely.
Ask that she duplicate material for everyone.	Women are helpers and assistants.	Request that this job be done on a rotating basis.
Ask her to arrange details for meetings (space, room, food).	Women are caretakers.	Request that these tasks be done on a rotating basis.
Over-react to a mistake.	Women are unreliable: what do you expect?	Give constructive feedback in the form of specific work-related examples regarding the implications of the mistake.

It was suggested earlier that our concepts of masculinity and femininity affect our behavior in several critical ways, especially our working behavior. They influence the response and treatment we expect from other people. They also affect the way we function in our roles and the way we behave toward the people who work with us. It follows then that the more an ordained male clarifies his own attitudes and expectations with regard to women, the better he will understand his behavior and the response it elicits from them.

Some of the forms these stereotypic views, attitudes, and behavior can take are depicted below. Do any of them sound familiar?

HOW SEX ROLE STEREOTYPES KEEP WOMEN DOWN[10]

MAN'S VIEW OF WOMEN	MAN'S ATTITUDE	MAN'S BEHAVIOR
1. As his grandmother	She's kindly and well-meaning, but . . .	Don't give her challenging, analytical tasks. Keep her out of the mainstream. Give her jobs where a mistake won't be costly.
2. As his mother	She takes care of our needs.	Give her people-oriented jobs. Keep her away from making decisions. Let her be a clerical assistant.
3. As his daughter	She needs protection.	Don't give her too much responsibility. Keep her out of the jobs where you need to be tough.
4. As a seductress	She'll distract me from my work.	Use her and fire her. Don't send her on the road.
5. As mother of the family	Her place is at home, not here.	Don't hire her; she'll just get married (have children) and leave.
6. As a protégé	She will go far.	Act as a teacher and guide (very rare).
7. As an intruder	She's not a member of the team.	Don't share data. Don't share inside information.
8. (Your examples)	(Your examples)	(Your examples)
9. (Your examples)	(Your examples)	(Your examples)

What Does All of This Mean
for the Future of the Church?

Working to eliminate the vestiges of clericalism and sexism will make it possible to employ more imaginative approaches to the pastoral work of the Church. New leadership styles can be utilized which will allow both men and women to responsibly participate in Church-related ministries.

Team ministry in its various developing models is one alternative form of pastoral leadership whereby the collegial vision of Vatican II may be implemented. To be sure, it is a dramatic departure from the hierarchical structure of the pre-Vatican II Church, and for this reason there is a tension for many ordained men today in trying to balance the "rugged individualists" they were conditioned to be with the "relational persons" shared ministry now urges them to be. Ministry requires a mature relationship between the ordained and unordained members of the team. Collegiality in a group can only be fostered through a relationship which is based on the reciprocal equality and mutuality of its members. Such "partnership" includes the whole range of the relationships and structures which denote reciprocity among people individually, between the sexes, between people and nature/cosmos, and, as the foundation of it all, between humankind and God. It does not mean the kind of relationship which subordinates one to another, nor that of "complementarity" which makes each tenaciously cling to his or her own particularities. What is meant here is a diversity of relationships which implies the mutual enrichment of each person.

The experience of the unordained women in the Church today is significantly different from that of ordained men. Ordained men are called to relinquish some of their hold on the ministerial tasks in the Church, while unordained women are challenged to assume a greater role in the leadership task of the Church. As long as men feel that the theological, pastoral and organizational skills they bring to ministry are being challenged or threatened by those they were trained to regard as their subordinates (and dependent on them for salvation!), it will be almost impossible for them to understand and accept women as ecclesial ministers.

Because Church order is historically constituted and in no way absolute, there must always be flexibility in the organization of Church ministries in order to meet continuing, new and practical demands of the Christian communities' efforts to live the mission and ministry of Jesus the Christ. And we can hope as well that in adjusting to new cultural situations, the Church will not be compromised by existing structures or ideologies.[11] Such hope can carry us as we strive toward genuine partnership in ministry. Letty M. Russell reminds us all that such partnership is possible when she writes:

> Partnership does have a future, just as it has a present and a past. It has a future because God has chosen to be partners with us, chosen to be present in our lives through Jesus Christ as a happening of co-humanity.[12]

What more convincing hope and trust could we have that partnership between ordained men and unordained women is possible?

NOTES

1. National Council of Catholic Bishops, *As One Who Serves: Reflections on the Pastoral Ministry of Priests in the United States* (Washington, D.C.: United States Catholic Conference, 1977), 35.

2. Many of these difficulties are addressed by Maria Harris in her article, "DRE's in the U.S.: The First Twenty Years," *The Living Light*, 17 (Fall 1980), pp. 250–259.

3. See Bernard Cooke, *Ministry to Word and Sacraments* (Philadelphia: Fortress, 1976), pp. 63–64, 205–206, 265–266.

4. Ida Raming, "From the Freedom of the Gospel to the Petrified 'Men's Church': The Rise and Development of Male Domination in the Church," *Women in a Men's Church*, Concilium, Virgil Elizondo and Norbert Greinacher, eds. (New York: Seabury, 1980), p. 3.

5. Doris Gottemoeller, "Women and Leadership in the Church," *New Catholic World* (Sept.-Oct. 1980), p. 202.

6. *Nonprofit Management Skills for Women Managers* (San Francisco: Public Management Institute, 1980), pp. 2–5.

7. Martina Horner, "Psychological Barriers to Achievement in Women," *Journal of Social Issues* (Vol. 28, 1972).

8. I. Broverman *et al.* "Sex Role Stereotypes and Clinical Judgments of Mental Health," *Journal of Consulting and Clinical Psychology* (February 1970).

9. *Nonprofit Management Skills for Women Managers,* pp. 24–25.

10. Adapted from "How Sex Role Stereotypes Keep Women Down," in *Nonprofit Management Skills for Women Managers,* pp. 30–31.

11. Margaret Brennan, "Women and Men in Church Office," *Women in a Men's Church,* p. 106.

12. Letty M. Russell, *The Future of Partnership* (Philadelphia: Westminster, 1979), p. 159.

The Nuns' Story

Joanmarie Smith

Without story our lives are, as William James would say, "a blooming, buzzing confusion." We see our existence in terms of beginnings, endings, dramatic turning points and numberless sub-plots. We have to. A life not lived in story form is meaningless, and our greatest human need seems to be for meaning. Consider the fallout in terror from an event which we cannot locate in terms of causes or implications.

In this essay, however, my concern is not so much with the individual narratives we live as with the story-framework within which we live them. This framework is variously called world-view, a life context or even one's metaphysics.

The degree to which we create our story or are created by it is one of the fundamental philosophical issues our story-framework handles. Plato, who posited a really real world apart from this world's "apparent" reality, would suggest that there is a blueprint of our story somewhere (in God's mind, according to Augustine). The extent to which we fill out the lines of this pre-existing story would then mark the extent to which we really become who we are. This Platonic philosophic framework was long the context of Western civilization's story. That context, however, began to be abandoned with increasing rapidity from the sixteenth century on. The Protestant Reformation and the rise of science in that era initiated the change embraced by modern Western thinkers with the exception of Roman Catholic thinkers. In fact, the Church seemed to laminate that framework for future generations of Catholics in its pronouncements from the Council of Trent.

Now, whatever the details of an individual's life story, their interpretation comes from these larger philosophical and/or theological frameworks. So, for example, in the Platonic framework, a great sorrow might take its meaning from the conviction that the sorrow represents God's will or at least God's permission, and the degree to which I accept or, even better, embrace this sorrow, to that degree will I conform to the form of me that God has in mind. To that degree will I become who I am. When I entered the convent thirty years ago, it was in this framework (the Plato part—not the sorrow part).

God's plan was that I become a Sister of St. Joseph. He called me, held out a vocation to me. And I answered that call. In the novitiate I was educated to what being a nun involved. One became a bride of Christ. The rule provided such a detailed blueprint for living out that title that lay persons could only envy us. "You keep the holy rule and the holy rule will keep you" was a frequently heard adage that made eminent sense to me then—in that framework; in fact, it still does—in that framework.

It is my impression that priests who entered the seminary at this same time were similarly educated—that they saw themselves in analogous terms and that their framework was characterized (as was ours) by stability, simplicity, and certitude. The framework was God-given and, therefore, changeless. They would be "priests forever." And there was no complexity about what that involved. Moreover, one could be certain that in obeying one's pastor or bishop one could do no wrong—even if the pastor's or bishop's orders were wrong (Shades of "You keep the rule and the rule will keep you"). Then a funny thing happened on the way from Vatican Council II.

Vatican II, of course, did not usher in the shift in framework; it simply crystallized the shift as a possibility. The question could now at least be posed: After the Galileo case, we no longer think that our act of faith commits us to a particular physics; must we still think that our faith commits us to a particular metaphysics? Theoretically, the jury is still out on that one. But, more and more, nuns have consciously or unconsciously changed their framework. For priests, the change has not been so easy or so widespread. It is my contention that the clash in frameworks has been the source of much of any conflict which exists between nuns and priests who must work together.

Nuns' Stories

The nuns' story began to change to a myriad of stories in the late 1960's. From 1965 to 1970, I taught in a sister formation college. Setting up these intercongregational institutions had the effect, first of all, of fostering relationships across congregational lines. It was simultaneously discovered that the differences among congregations was minuscule. In fact, any differences stemmed more from the different personalities at the helm of the order than from differing philosophies or theologies informing them. An even more important effect was the focused inquiry that was promoted among these young women. During a council when the Church was questioning its own identity, no area was beyond the pale of investigation. In the fall-out from that period, nuns' stories changed radically. Among those who entered the convent from 1960 to 1975, approximately two-thirds have left. The median age of my own congregation is, at this time, fifty-six and rising! Those who stayed began to live a different story-framework—a story now characterized by uncertainty, complexity, and instability.

Uncertainty

One of the most prominent features of this new story-framework is that it lacks a neat theology of what it is to be a nun. The bride of Christ theology, except in the most conservative congregations, disappeared somewhat in the way the ideology of indulgences did. People just stopped using the term and the trappings that reinforced it. There were no more wedding gowns at the reception of postulants into the novitiate, no more books or hymns about "sponsae Christi." The vows themselves became problematic.

Poverty is an evil. The dilemma is obvious. To embrace what is universally seen to be an evil smacks of masochism. On the other hand, to call the relatively middle-class security that most congregations enjoy "poverty" smacks of obscenity. In the old context, fidelity to the vow had hinged on permission. Poverty was equated with dependence. The ideal of dependence was subverted by studies into the psychology of maturity. Independence and interdependence are the values pursued by actualizing adults. Simultaneously, the incongruity of a situation where one thinks oneself poor yet could study abroad, take trips, have a car for personal use, etc., as long as one had permission, became apparent. The new interpretation of poverty is simplicity. Members of congregations are enjoined to simplify their lives as much as possible—an ideal, it must be noted, enjoined not only on all Christians but upon everyone as the world's population increases and its resources decrease. That left obedience and chastity as the defining notes of women in religious orders.

I sometimes mark the unraveling of the theology of sisterhood in my religious congregation with a letter from the motherhouse saying that a sister could take a walk around the block without asking the superior. We had been taught that obedience was the linchpin of our religious vocation. Obviously the other two vows could be absorbed by it. We heard that, in fact, there were some congregations who "took" only the vow of obedience. If the bell calling us to prayer or work or recreation was considered "the voice of God," how much more so were the superior's words. God spoke through her so that anything she enjoined was God's will for us. Moreover, anything we asked to do and were permitted to do then became blessed by the assurance that it, too, was God's will. In that context, then, it was not at all absurd that in my congregation, once a month, the sisters would gather in their convents to ask permission "to pass from one part of the house to another, to wash and mend our clothes. . . ." Such an exercise ever more closely allied our lives with our "calling." But if one could walk around the block without permission, why couldn't one go home to visit the family without permission? Or, for that matter, why couldn't one go to Europe? With that letter from the motherhouse, therefore, the toothpaste started coming out of the tube, as it were. And it became impossible to put it back—at least it would not go back into the same tube.

The period from the change that this letter presaged to its verbalization in the documents of the congregation seemed endless at the time. In retrospect, however, the shift occurred with marvelous speed. Our temporary "rule" (an interesting juxtaposition of terms) still speaks of discerning God's will (there's still a blueprint somewhere), but now describes this will being made known "in a multiplicity of ways—in prayer, Scripture, personal events, the needs of our time, dialogue with the sisters with whom we live, with those in authority and the people to whom we minister." In addition, in the section where the rule treats of obedience, the emphasis is on personal decisions, responsibility and dialogue. The rule no longer "keeps us." The certitude is gone. What is left, then, to mark off the vocation? Chastity?

But chastity is also a human value. To be respectful and modest—in the richest senses of those terms—toward oneself and others is, again, a value of personhood, not specifically of persons in religious orders. Not so celibacy. The Jews remind us that the *very* first commandment is to increase and multiply (Gen. 1:28)—a commandment most people are happy to obey. To forego fulfilling this commandment is unique in the universe. Such a stance remarkably specifies a group who embraces it. It is not surprising, then, that "chastity" like "bride of Christ" has disappeared from our vocabulary. Celibacy has replaced it. At this critical point our lives overlap those of priests. There is a crucial difference, however. Celibacy is not an essential note of priesthood. It is grounded in an historical necessity. As such, it is recognized as purely disciplinary, and most theologians agree that the celibacy requirement in the Roman rite will, in the future, become as optional as it has always been in the Eastern rite. With nuns, however, a paradox has arisen. More and more, celibacy has become the specifying note of their vocation. This has the effect of having one's identity based on a sexual anomaly. Of course, there is nothing wrong with that if you can ground the value of the situation in a compelling framework. My constitutions speak of celibacy freeing the sister "to respond to God and his people with her entire sensitivity and affectivity." At first reading this seems obvious enough. Yet, it seems to me, there is an unfortunate implication embedded in such thinking. It overlooks the fact that most of the most dramatic service to humanity is rendered by married persons—doctors, statesmen, religious missionaries of other communions, among them. Such oversight neglects the common wisdom that their service is energized and enhanced in and by their marriage. Another form of the implication might go: If celibacy is freeing, sex must be a drag—literally and figuratively.

Not all the theory of celibacy is in that bag, however. There is also the thesis that celibacy acts as a sign in this world of the eschaton. "By the consecration of her entire humanity, with all that this implies for her as a woman, she is a sign of the transcendence of God calling her and all people to the fullness of life—total union with him." This may, of course, be the case, but it does seem that a radical commitment to justice could serve similarly, if not so uniquely, as that sign. But if celibacy were no longer held as a specifying note of what it means to be a nun, what would be left? That question anguishes many of us today. But some have learned not simply to live with the ambiguity of our situation, but to embrace it as the human condition because they have completely abandoned the old framework or paradigm against which they previously lived out their stories. Ambiguity has replaced certitude as the primary color of their lives. However, an even more fascinating characteristic of life in religious orders today is that sisters with different contexts can live in the same congregation and even, at times, side by side.

Complexity

A different context changes not only the text of a story but also its texture. The different frameworks that brace the various members' stories produce a complex living situation. The dress of the members is a dramatic signal of more profound diversity within religious orders. I imagine that my own congregation is similar to many others in having within its ranks women who still wear a habit whose fundamentals can be traced back centuries. Other women wear what is termed "the modified habit." (An interesting aside on the modified habit: they are, for the most part, indistinguishable congregationally; that is, the dress that was once so distinctive for each religious order has been replaced by a uniform that simply signals "nun" with no further qualifications. In this our garb resembles the Roman collar.) Still other women are in various renditions of contemporary dress variously secured from such disparate places as thrift shops and Bonwit Teller.

Such diversity dramatically reflects the multiplicity of stories being lived simultaneously. Most of the communities in my congregation operate without a superior. The buck of responsibility for these communities stops at each sister. The style and content of our prayer life is also the responsibility of the local community, and each sister shapes her spirituality in the light of the local decision. We group and determine how the money which comes into the house will be dispersed after we pay our tax to the larger congregation. We also choose our work, our living situation. The complexity that such variety introduces into the congregation as a whole and into each local community, potentially at least, enriches the texture of our lives or, to use Whitehead's term, the intensity. Harmony in music provides a fruitful analogy. The texture and richness of a harmony depends upon the quality and spread of the notes. Any single note that becomes another or is not "true" to its identity diminishes the entire harmony.

But nuns must now face the dawning realization that with such ambiguity in defining ourselves and with such an assortment of life styles (with the exception of celibacy) we may not really be a unique entity after all. The question is endemic to nuns' meetings: "What is the essence of religious life?" The anguish of the question is exacerbated by those persons (especially those women who have left religious orders) who justifiably take umbrage at our equating *religious* life with life in a religious order. It seems that whatever we are doing as nuns we could readily do as "women in the world." We know this to be so because, more often than not, we are already doing whatever we are doing with "women in the world." In the light of these realities, and faced with the statistics of decreasing numbers and an increasing median age, members of religious order are having to learn to live with an instability more profound than economic anxiety. It is the instability introduced in the face of ultimately losing one's identity—of dying.

Instability

People die, and institutions die, of course, but they are other people, other institutions. In the past ten years, nuns have had to confront, with varying degrees of consciousness and with varying degrees of success, the possible (some would say "imminent") death of nunhood as an institution. In a way, it's easier to accept the inevitability that one's own life will end than the inevitability that the institution in which one has lived this life will end. A frequently heard comment on this situation goes "Well, religious life as we know it may change, but it will survive in some form." This may, in fact, be the case, or it may be an advanced form of denial, the first stage of the response to dying.

Then there is the danger of self-fulfilling prophecy. We may not be dying, but sounding the death knell will certainly discourage any vibrant young women from joining us. It is an especially acute sorrow to think of the possible death of an institution which can now, more than ever, offer both its members and those it serves such a maturing and rich existence. And so it goes.

The Priests' Story

I cannot, obviously, recount the priests' story. I can only indicate how I read it. For centuries, we shared the same framework. We both knew with certitude what a nun was and what a priest was. We got along better then because we both "knew our place" and stayed in it. Our stories were simple and stable. Now, as the burden of this essay has been at pains to demonstrate, nuns no longer know their place—literally and figuratively. The effect of the shift has been to exasperate both parties. Priests seem to be threatened and angry with the demand for equal billing that some nuns put forth in their parishes. The sisters, on the other hand, have in many cases become impatient to the point of bitterness at the intransigence of pastors.

But priests are, I think, in another ballgame. The identity of nuns involved who they were, not what they did. Priests' identity however is very much caught up in what they can do. Most dramatically, they can celebrate Mass and hear confessions. *But,* and it is a very big *but,* the power to exercise these functions requires the permission of a bishop. That is, although nominally a priest by ordination, each ordained man must depend for his faculties on a bishop—who is appointed, not elected, appointed by the Pope who himself was elected by bishops (at the level of cardinal)—who had been appointed by a Pope, etc. It is difficult in such a procedure to cultivate other world-views or different contexts for one's story. The practical consequence of this situation is that the very identity of a cleric—that is, his power to function—is in the hands and world-view of his "boss." Another consideration is that while education for the priesthood is, on one level, infinitely broadening, on another it is so limiting as to keep priests "in their places" for practical economic reasons. Saying Mass and hearing confessions are not particularly marketable skills. A priest's faculties, then, are also the source of his livelihood. A bishop's hold on his priests is understandable, if not enviable. Ironically, the priests, who from nuns' pre-Vatican II vantage point seemed to have so much more freedom than we did, now seem to have so much less. Perhaps the wonder is that there is not greater antagonism between us.

I hope I have not caricatured the priests' story or obscured the main point of this essay, to wit: It is not the picayune issues that are the source of much of the antagonism between priests and nuns in the same ministry, but rather the differing frameworks or world-views within which they shape their respective stories. But there are many kinds of stories.

A Typology of Story

John Dominic Crossan speaks of five types of stories and their relationship to the world. *Myth* establishes world. *Apologue* defends world. *Action* investigates world. *Satire* attacks world. *Parable* subverts world. What I have been calling framework or context or world-view is what Crossan calls myth. He speaks of myth as that which structures relations. Myth structures our world.

Crossan quickly moves through those story types which defend or investigate or attack world to the form which is his main focus: parable—which shatters our myths. In the past fifteen years, biblical scholars in general have concentrated their various analytic tools on the parables of Jesus. Whatever their approach, there is some consensus that parable requires us to question our most basic conceptions about reality. This is certainly Crossan's approach. He calls parable the dark night of story. I am suggesting that, perhaps, if nuns and priests can't share the same story/myth, they can share the same story/parable.

To inhabit parable requires, most fundamentally, a recognition that our frameworks, whether characterized by certainty or uncertainty, simplicity or complexity, stability or changelessness, are not the last word. To inhabit parable seems to require the further recognition that there may be no last word.

Parable is so shattering because it canonizes no framework. It suggests, moreover, that there is no framework. Crossan, at one point, describes a typical reaction to parable: "I don't know what you mean by the story but I'm certain I don't like it." He makes a strong case for his conviction that in most places the evangelists redacted the parabolic sayings and stories of Jesus into less scandalous, less disturbing examples or allegories. For example, he hypothesizes that the various renditions of the saying in Matthew 25:29, Mark 4:25, Matthew 13:12 and Luke 8:18 were originally: "To him who has will be given; from him who has not will be taken away." But who can make sense of that? For Crossan, such reinterpretation is legitimate because the cross replaced the parables and became, in their place, the supreme parable. The parables themselves, no longer the center, were freed to become examples and allegories—otherwise they would have been lost to us forever. Crossan concludes: "Jesus died as parabler and rose as Parable."

How, then, does one live in parable? To paraphrase an old joke, "Very painfully." But living in a parable is no joke. Yet, and here comes the parabolic part: if, as I have hypothesized, so much of any antagonism that exists between nuns and priests comes from our separate myths, I propose that our meetings in parable be characterized, not by prayer (though that is always an option), but by laughter.

Laughter is the appropriate response to a good joke. And nothing in our experience comes closer to the parable than the joke. The essence of both is that they shatter our expectation. Incongruity is their hallmark. Maybe nuns and priests can meet in the paradox of the profound ambiguity and unfreedom they experience in a life lived in and for the liberating Logos.

Laughter is also a peculiarly human response. *Homo ridens* is as specifying as *homo sapiens*. Apparently, only humans, those meaning-makers, can detect the ridiculous and react, not with fear, nor with anguish, nor even with sorrow, but with a hearty laugh. (Ridiculous comes from the same root, ridere—to laugh.) It's intriguing. Perhaps that most fundamental human need for meaning is not necessary after all, or perhaps we can transcend our most fundamental needs. Perhaps it is in this mode that we are made in God's image.

What, then, am I suggesting? That nuns and priests sit around and swap jokes or watch old Marx Brothers movies? Not quite—though that is another good option. But I think our time would be even better spent swapping stories that reflect the incongruity of our lives. And the first one to laugh wins.

What is won? The realization that "God does not play by our rules," and the experience of a deep and unique freedom. Laughter is some kind of ultimate letting-go. One can clutch things while crying, but laughter is relaxing and expanding. To laugh and grasp is all but impossible. Laughter wins companionship, too. Try to hate or be angry with someone with whom you have laughed. I'll bet you can't. But be forewarned: Sometimes laughter looks like crying.

The Ordained Woman: Embarrassment or Gift?

Karen Bloomquist

It is June 1980 in St. Patrick's Cathedral, New York City. The occasion is an historic Lutheran-Roman Catholic celebration. Hundreds of clergy process down the aisle. Suddenly stunned glances, nervous nudges, and smiles of both incredulity and support surface in the congregation, for in the procession are a half dozen women vested in the usual clerical garb.

We are marching in a hierarchical, patriarchal procession. That is perilous. It can either swallow us up *or* our presence might provoke questions as to its very legitimacy. This reflects the difficult tension facing most clergywomen. There is much in the clergy "caste" system that we find oppressive, but we have chosen, usually with considerable ambivalence, to live out our calling in some relation to it, with the sometimes foolish hope of transforming it in the process.

We are fully ordained ministers and are becoming an increasingly visible component. Para-military and Pentecostal churches have had the largest percentage of female clergy. Today in addition to well over two hundred of us in North American Lutheran churches there are thousands in other mainline denominations. Master of Divinity classes in many Protestant seminaries are one-third to one-half female. Our numbers have rapidly escalated in the past decade. We are found in most mainline denominations in this country with the major exceptions being the Orthodox, Lutheran Church-Missouri Synod, and Roman Catholic churches. We are single and married, widows and divorcées, mothers and grandmothers. We serve congregations as solo pastors, assistants or associates, and even as senior pastors. We minister on campuses, in hospitals, in community agencies, in denominational offices (including as "bishop"), and in previously overlooked centers of need such as battered women's shelters. Some of us are in team ministries with our husbands; others minister separately from them. In some cases the style and emphases of our ministries are little different from that of men, but in many instances the weave and texture of ministry is changing because of our presence.

Our presence as ordained ministers of the church is often treated as an ecumenical embarrassment vis-à-vis churches that do not ordain women. We are the "lump" that gets stuck in the throat of such ecumenical conversations. When the possibility of mutually-recognized ministry is raised in official dialogues we are kept out of sight. Doctrinal foundations for agreement are to be ironed out first. Only after that will differences in practice be addressed. But is such a dichotomy valid? Liberation theologians would challenge such a theory-practice split. So does the flesh-and-blood presence of ordained women. Our participation in ordained ministry needs to be included in emergent doctrines of ministry. It is naive to assume that doctrinal consensus arrived at by males can lead to anything other than a male norm for the practice of ordained ministry. The terms are established in a way that *a priori* excludes women's experience. Thus we become an anomaly that does not quite fit the norm.

Not only do ordained women need to be included in ecumenical discussions, but the heart of what feminist theology is about needs to be taken more seriously. Theology arises out of concrete, lived experience. Thus in discussing the ordination of women, instead of beginning with the endless speculative debates as to whether or not women can be ordained—arguments which usually are pre-determined by one's own position on the subject—why not begin with the actual experiences of real-life clergywomen, with the concrete and experiential rather than the abstractly speculative? What "theology of ministry" is emerging in albeit fragile glimpses from out of the experience of women in ministry? How can this become a gift rather than an embarrassment in ecumenical relationships with those church bodies that do not yet ordain women?

An ordained woman is likely to have experienced some opposition, resistance and prejudice. Aspersions are sometimes cast on her sense of call to ministry: "She wants to be a man . . . she's trying prove something . . . she's motivated more by feminism than by a theological sense of call." The woman often finds herself in a Catch-22 situation. She should be neither too much "like a man" (too aggressive) nor too much "like a woman" (too soft). If she pursues her calling to ordained ministry she at some point encounters resistance due to her "lack of fit" in this pervasively male-defined role—which doesn't "fit" for some men either! This may take the form of an outright prohibition or a more unconscious resistance to the full acceptance of her as pastor/priest. In any case it is likely to provoke a certain amount of anger. If this is expressed, she is viewed as "an angry woman," ergo unfit for the ordained ministry. If it goes unexpressed she either tacitly consents to the exclusion or is grudgingly incorporated as no different from "one of the guys."

Although there are vast differences in the amount of resistance a clergywoman may have experienced, there is general agreement that *some* male clergy colleagues as well as those in authority over her are likely to be greater problems than are the laity. The reasons for this, many of them deeply psychological, need much further exploration. Because men who enter the ministry are viewed already as somewhat "feminine" by society, their anxiety mounts when they actually see a woman in that same role. Rosemary Ruether has suggested that the fear of women as priests resides in the maternal archetypes related to sacramentality. The female priest challenges it as a male role and evokes a return of that which is repressed.[1] Male clergy who understand and feel comfortable with their own sexuality and who are not afraid to embrace "feminine" qualities are more likely to be accepting of female colleagues. Those who are not are likely to pass their resistance and fear on to the laity.

Lay resistance to the ordination of women has often been shaped by male clergy, but when laity personally experience the ministry of a woman their resistance tends to dissipate. An elderly woman of Russian Orthodox background came to me a year after I had become her pastor to confess her sin and plead for my forgiveness. Her "sin" was that she had harbored resistance against a woman being her "priest" because of how deeply male priests had ingrained in her the taboo against a woman even entering the chancel during her menstrual period, much less serving as a priest! "My sin was in allowing that taboo to stand in the way. . . . I now fully accept you as my priest, because I have come to know you as a person," she declared. In countless cases, even conservative laity who are opposed to the *abstract idea* of an "ordained woman" change their attitude quickly when they experience the *actual* presence and ministry of an ordained woman.

Dwelling on the prohibitions and resistance toward the ordination of women can deter consideration of what it is that ordained women are embodying in ministry already. These are not necessarily stereotypical feminine qualities. Women may feel freer to embody certain nurturing, feeling qualities than do men because of our social conditioning. But men as well as women can and do embody these. Some clergywomen may be stronger and more assertive than some men—they have *had* to be in order to survive! We are not necessarily better with small children, nor are we always the best counselors for women. We may in some instances be the better administrators, preachers and liturgical leaders. Generally our gifts and strengths are as varied as men's.

Just as there is a danger of stereotyping the qualities women bring to the ministry, so we must also guard against romanticizing what women will be or do. In ministry situations that are not flourishing, such as "marginal" congregations, there is a tendency to hope that women will be able to do what men have failed to do—"save the church" (usually said only half-seriously). Not only does this lapse into assuming that the body of Christ needs "saving," but it also sets women up for rather unrealistic expectations. If in two years she has not "rescued" the congregation, some who were skeptical at first may have their suspicions confirmed: "See, we should have stayed with a man!"

Women do seem to serve a disproportionate number of "dying, marginal" congregations which in many cases cannot afford a "real" pastor. They are not necessarily effecting dramatic changes in these situations, but frequently they are affirming and raising up new symbols of hope among the people. One can sense a new-found sense of identity and spirit in older, ethnic, working-class congregations that may be nearly written off by denominational leaders but are pastored by new, energetic clergywomen. There often is at least an initial freedom to do things differently than did their male predecessors. Women are not belabored by the usual role expectations in quite the same way.

There is a sense in which women's "lack of fit" in the role of pastor/priest can be something of an asset. It may provide new possibilities of entree into people's lives. The traditional women's circles rank low in priority and are treated patronizingly or with half-seriousness by many clergymen. They feel awkwardly out-of-place in such settings. Yet the chitchat that goes on here can be richly disclosive of what people really are feeling. Here they share with one another aspects of their lives that would never get shared with male pastors. The same is true for the reminiscing that goes on in senior citizens' gatherings. Grace flows through the inter-connections they make with one another. When I, a female pastor, am present in such settings, the perception that I am "one of them" is stronger than the set-apartness of my role as pastor. Generally I am experienced as being less obtrusive to that group's dynamics and thus can be privy to much that would ordinarily be closed off to the "pastor." Obviously there are many nuns and lay women in ministry who experience a similar phenomenon and do a lot of ministering in those contexts. But a woman who is also their pastor/priest can embody a crucial link from that setting to the Sunday service. The experiences and pain expressed in that setting are usually set apart from what occurs on Sunday morning, or treated as data irrelevant to the "real" business of the church. Because of the dual way I am perceived—as a woman *and* as their pastor—I can help bridge that gap. What goes on in the sacraments has a touchstone with what went on in that "coffee klatch." The word and sacraments begin to permeate the common ordinary segments of life. Making these kinds of connections has been a most meaningful aspect of ministry for me.

Some clergywomen have used "midwife" imagery to describe their style of ministry. In settings such as the above, a midwife who stands alongside, encouraging people as they give birth to themselves in new ways, is perhaps more appropriate than an "obstetrician" who artificially "induces delivery" in the confessional or study.

Men's lives also may be touched in new ways by clergywomen. In a society where male expressions of weakness or vulnerability have traditionally been scorned, some find it easier to reveal such to a woman. Perhaps she reminds him of the mother before whom tears could flow. One elderly, candid parishioner whom I had helped through the grief process after the loss of his wife turned to me and said, "Pastor, I didn't know what it would feel like to have a woman for my pastor, but it feels good. You've been kind of like a 'mother' to me, and that's what a pastor should be like. I don't know if I'd want to go back to having a man for a pastor!" I don't really want to be thought of as "mother" but what is important to recognize is that this retired working man had experienced a much different dynamic which he valued, and his image of "pastor" had consequently shifted dramatically.

As a parish pastor one is invited into people's most intimate, critical moments of life and death. At such *kairos* times, people are stripped of masks and defenses, yet because they feel so vulnerable they often respond in stilted, stereotyped ways. The pastor/priest usually symbolizes stability and reassurance in such moments, reminding people of the upholding presence of an unchanging God. Through such means as the clerical collar, clergywomen also symbolize this stability. However, it is combined with elements of surprise, change and incongruity. Our presence tends to break up images and stereotyped responses. Because people usually expect to relate to a clergy*man* at this point in their lives, they experience a fleeting but jarring disorientation.

If God is defined in traditionally male terms and the priest is expected to signify or "resemble" this God (as in the 1976 Vatican Declaration against the ordination of women), women are *ipso facto* excluded. Most Protestants would resist the notion of the pastor signifying who God is. Nevertheless, people's image of God often is subtly connected with who their pastor is and does seem to shift as they experience the ministry of women. God becomes more than an unchanging God of stability. God is also one who surprises and disorients us, provoking us to look in new ways at the One who we assumed was unchanging. The old assumptions regarding how things "have to be" begin to crack, and through the cracks God's grace begins to flow anew. Things don't *have* to be the way we thought they were. Priests aren't necessarily male; God isn't necessarily unchanging. The givens of life are not inevitable. Change and reorientation is possible in ways that can open up new dimensions of who God is—and of who we are.

It is in this incongruity or synapse between the expected and the unexpected, the image and the reality, that we catch glimmers of the inbreaking of God's mystery, grace and presence. This is a sacramental moment. Those whom we have not expected to be bearers of God's presence—like Sarah and Mary—become that for us, in variance with what we have known to be "the sacred tradition." It is in the jarring that God wakes us up and speaks to us in new tones. The tradition is still there and important for grounding what we are about, but the mysterious dynamic of the Spirit is experienced in the tension of the old with the new. This "space" is a fragile moment which will no longer be incongruous and jarring when "woman" and "pastor/priest" become increasingly more compatible in our social imagery and reality.

This suggests a different view of priesthood, similar to that developed by Urban Holmes. The priest is not one who controls or produces predictable results, but is the liminal or threshold person who stands between structure and anti-structure, a *mana*-person who is in touch with that which seems chaotic and diabolic.[2] Clergywomen present an unusual combination of the traditional and unexpected, akin to the life-transforming dynamic of Pentecost. It is a dynamic that those traditionally in authority do not know what to do about, for it has a power and depth that alternatively allures and resists, provokes and reassures, transforms and stabilizes. It is pregnant with new expressions of the holy.

Except for Episcopalians, most denominations that ordain women shy away from a focus on the priestly dimension. Ministry of the word tends to be emphasized instead. The evangelical understanding of ordained ministry is not intended to be hierarchical but functional on behalf of the priesthood of all believers. The pastor is not different in being nor graced with a special essence. He or she is called or set apart to *do* certain things rather than to *be* something special. Thus there should be less of a tendency to see the pastor as separated, distanced or different from the people. Such understandings of ministry have perhaps made it easier theologically to accept the ordination of women. But as women function in the ordained role, it is especially in the priestly/sacramental dimension that some different nuances emerge. Although women's entree into ordained ministry may be through the more word-oriented traditions, it may be the more sacramental emphases that are especially affected.

No matter how strongly it is insisted that the function does not depend on the person—that she is merely filling an office that men usually have in the past—nevertheless, what the woman *as person* brings to that role/office cannot be ignored. Her presence in that ordained role stirs us to the realization that the "who-ness" *is* important. Who one *is* and what one *does* cannot be split asunder. The richness of that person with all the intricate everyday webs in which her life is caught up is not separable from those acts which are unique and central to her priestly functions. Sacred and profane functions of life are co-mingled. Who she is as priest cannot be fully appreciated apart from who she is as a person.

Sociologists as well as theologians might cringe at such a merging of roles or confusion of person and role. Yet as clergywomen talk among themselves (such support groups are essential!), it is amazing to what degree our personal and professional lives are intermeshed. Caring for one's sick child, fixing breakfast, leading a Bible study group, contacting the community board, finding food for the hungry man, fixing the plumbing, counseling the grieving widow, doing the banking, hearing a friend's or husband's tale of woe, writing the sermon and celebrating the Eucharist can all be a part of one's jumbled day. One activity merges into another. Admittedly, a male cleric's day can be just as frenetic! But in our society men's professional lives have been seen as more segregated or distanced from their personal lives. Women typically have had to juggle many diverse threads of life at once. Even if a woman is single she seldom has the luxury of being able to focus all her energy at one time on her professional responsibilities or calling. She doesn't have a wife or housekeeper to tend to all those other concerns.

All this can become nerve-wracking and energy-draining and is often viewed as detrimental to one's professional dedication. Certainly questions can be raised as to the justice of women's being expected to carry so many family/home responsibilities in addition to their professional calling. However, I maintain that all these strands and strains of life become a part of the fabric that is involved in the sacramental action. To carry within oneself such diverse experiences of life—the loftiest and the lowliest—is to embody a sacrament within the Sacrament. Those who commune are reminded of new aspects of the ordinariness of life that are touched and transformed by the Real Presence. It is in the celebrant's words that Christ and the community meet and commune. But that meeting has a different nuance and texture because of the experiences constituting the "who" that speaks the words.

Ordaining women is more than a matter of simple justice or equal rights. The inclusiveness of the Church, the Gospel and the sacraments is at stake. If women are excluded from the central word and act of the Church, how is its inclusiveness, meaning and power for *all* people but especially women compromised? What nuances of experience remain untouched by its transforming power? Who or what is impoverished? How do our images of God become idolatrized—and our metaphors of human experience become too narrow? How does the refusal to include women in that speaking and acting distort our theology?

The question is not whether women can be ordained, but whether the Church can afford *not* to if it is to be faithful to the Gospel it is called to proclaim and embody.

I carry within me a pain for my sisters for whom the above connecting and embodying is not a recognized reality, despite their calling, and for their brothers and sisters who are thus cut off from the word and act of these women. But I also carry a hope that what has already been birthed through women proclaiming and celebrating will continue to grow as an ecumenical gift, not an embarrassment to be aborted.

In April 1980 over one hundred clergywomen were gathered in the chapel of a Roman Catholic retreat center, there celebrating the Eucharist. What a joyful, empowering celebration it was, as we experienced together the old yet suddenly new meanings of that ancient meal! It was a truly sacred moment. With arms linked together we jubilantly recessed down the aisle dancing. Suddenly I looked up. There in the gallery we were encircled by nuns, clapping and singing with us in celebration of the "already-not-yet" being born in the "womb" of their chapel. That symbol of hope empowers and sustains me.

NOTES

1. Rosemary Radford Ruether, "Why Males Fear Women Priests," *The Witness* 63:7 (July 1980), p. 21.

2. Urban T. Holmes, III, *Ministry and Imagination* (New York: Seabury, 1976), pp. 221–222.

Women in Judaism: Toward a Universal Humanity

Edith Wyschogrod

Women in Jewish life like those of other faiths are doubly bonded: to those in their faith communities and to other women transcending communal lines. But contemporary Jewish experience is unique in that the national trauma of the holocaust has altered the character of communal bonding and given it a primacy that may transcend sexual identity. At the same time the cultural and institutional frame of reference which determines the status of women in religious life is still both in obvious and in subtle ways derived from classical Judaism. Thus the Jewish woman is confronted with two powerful and, in many contexts, opposed identity creating experiences: anti-semitism and anti-feminism. In the attempt to respond to one she may inevitably lapse into ignoring the significance of the other. This is an especially pernicious state of affairs if she decides upon a feminist course of action, for she may then feel that she is undermining a sense of unity in a community whose annihilation in our time had very nearly become a reality. This sense of guilt is meta-psychological: it is not experienced as guilt feeling but as straying from a fundamental tenet of Judaism—loyalty to the covenant community. However, once these tensions are understood as part of a theological rather than a psychological problematic, their meaning can be explored in terms of the categories of Jewish theological self-interpretation: sin and repentance, God's justice and mercy, exile and return. I shall turn first to a brief account of the position of women in normative Judaism in order to make plain the clash in sensibilities experienced by women who wish to remain committed to some form of Jewish religious life and contemporary culture. I shall then turn to the several theological accounts of the holocaust which have dominated contemporary Jewish reflection upon this experience. In this way I hope to place the theme of women's desire for full participation in the structures of ritual and communal experience and the nadir experience of the holocaust side by side. In the concluding section I hope to suggest some general principles drawn from modern and post-modern Jewish theology from which guidelines for resolving the dilemma confronted by Jewish women might be drawn. Thus, I shall not suggest specific juridical principles which might be usefully employed in altering specific interpretations of the legislation governing the religious life of women in normative Judaism. To be sure such analysis is useful and considerable progress has already been made in this direction. Instead I shall try to pick out what I believe to be the underlying thread which unites disparate Jewish theologies and to suggest how this unitary strain might establish a starting point for the resolution of the theological crisis confronting Jewish women.

Women in Normative Judaism

The *locus classicus* of the traditional attitude toward women in normative Judaism is to be found in the rabbinic commentaries on Genesis 1:27 and Genesis 2:21–24. Rabbinic anthropology interprets the two versions of the creation narrative as reflecting the twofold nature of man: man as a corporeal being is fashioned from the dust of the earth while man as a spiritual being is made after the image of God.[1] The creation of woman also reflects this dualistic perspective. From the spiritual point of view woman is created in the image of God:

> So God created man in his own image; in the image of God created he him; male and female he created them (Gen. 1:27).

But physically woman is shaped from a part of man's body:

> And so the Lord God put the man into a trance, and
> while he slept, he took one of his ribs and closed the
> flesh over the place. The Lord God then built up into a
> woman the rib he had taken out of the man. He
> brought her to the man and the man said
>> "Now this at last
>> Is bone from my bones
>> And flesh from my flesh!
>> This shall be called woman
>> For from man was she taken."
> That is why a man leaves his father and mother and is
> united to his wife and the two become one flesh" (Gen.
> 2:21–24).

The rabbis interpret the latter text as an aetiological narrative
accounting for the institution of marriage. Marriage is not es-
sentially a contractual but rather a natural relation, part of the
plan of Providence ("That is why a man leaves his father and
mother and is united to his wife and the two become one flesh").
Etymological evidence is adduced for this conclusion: "And he
called his wife Eve for she was the mother of life."

Rabbinic interpretation of the former text (Gen. 1:27) suggests that the first person was an androgyne.[2] But such a being
complete in itself would lack selflessness, compassion and gener-
osity. God therefore divides the person into male and female:
neither is self-sufficient; each requires the other for completion:

> Had God created man and woman from the earth each
> independently, each would have gone his own way.
> Husband and wife would not be designated one for the
> other to live together.... Rather God created woman
> from man so that they should live together as one unit,
> each one needing the other.[3]

This understanding of creation establishes a framework in
which the family is the basic unit of society while marriage and

motherhood are the basic *religious* tasks of women. Together
with the synagogue and the school, the home is the center of religious instruction and liturgical life, the center for the powerful celebrations of joy, the sabbath and the Passover. A
frequently cited ideal is that of the *havil*, the woman of valor:

> Who can find a capable wife?
> Her worth is far beyond coral.
> Her husband's whole trust is in her.
> And the children are not lacking.
> She repays him good, not evil
> All her life long (Prov. 31:10–16).

Still the highest ideal of religious life is the study of Torah.
Such study is however reserved for men, and among men it is
restricted to a spiritual and intellectual elite. Women are exempt
from the command to engage in Torah learning. The Mishnah
states:

> Ben Azzai said that a man must teach his daughter To-
> rah. R. Eliezer said that he who teaches his daughter
> Torah has taught her *tiflut*.[5]

The term *tiflut* may be interpreted to mean "trivial and irrelevant things" or "immorality."[6] In the first interpretation wom-
en are seen as capable of only superficial knowledge; the second
indicates that such superficial knowledge could lead to immorality. The injunction against permitting women to study Torah
produces the paradoxical result that on the one hand, since the
study of Torah is always meritorious, women are rewarded for
its study (though to a lesser degree than men since they are not
divinely commanded to do so) and, on the other, they are in
practice discouraged from such study. The function of marriage
and child-rearing, not the study of Torah, is the designated
province of women.

Marriage itself is governed by the levitical laws of purity,
laws dealing with the menstruating woman. The rabbinic interpretation of the levitical law declares that the sexual act is for-

bidden during the menstrual period and for a week thereafter. The period of abstinence is followed by ritual immersion.[7] The regulations of menstrual impurity are set in two quite different teleological contexts. On the one hand woman is understood simply as a source of impurity and is seen to confer ritual pollution; on the other the period of separation is interpreted as a challenge to man's ability to obey the divine commandment.[8] A twelfth-century authority writes:

> And so that man should know that there is a God who rules over him, he has set for him laws and restrictions in his relationship with his wife, as he has set for him laws and restrictions in all other gifts that he has been given. [An enumeration of gifts follows.] Also to the gift of marriage he has given commandments.[9]

Normative Judaism reflects the severity of the original levitical legislation side by side with the rabbinic elaborations of these commandments which interpret the restrictive aspects of the original laws as manifestations of grace since they provide man with the opportunity to serve God through self-restraint.

Should a woman wish to terminate a marriage, divorce proceedings can only be initiated by the husband. This is at least part of the result of the nature of contracts in Judaic law. Since all contracts are unilateral, the divorce can only be initiated by one party.[10] A text from the period of formative Judaism reads:

> The woman is acquired by three means and she gains her freedom by two methods. She is acquired by money or document or sexual connection. . . . And she recovers her freedom by a letter of divorce or on the death of her husband.[11]

This interpretation is an adumbration of the principle stated in Deuteronomy 22:13 which rules that man is the initiator of the contract. While, according to rabbinic law, divorce is initiated by the husband, there is some protection for the woman in the marriage contract in that her husband can be forced to pay at least one year's support for his divorced wife, although many conditions are stipulated which could prevent such payment from being made.[12] A woman who seeks divorce can, under given conditions, appeal to a rabbinic court to exert pressure upon a reluctant husband to initiate divorce proceedings. But a woman is not free to remarry unless she is a widow or her husband has granted her a divorce. Thus for a woman whose marriage has terminated in fact but not in law (an *agunah*, literally a chained woman) obtaining a divorce is of considerable importance.[13] For those whose husbands refuse to grant a divorce or whose husbands have disappeared but cannot be proven dead, remarriage is impossible.

Apart from the special problems connected with marriage, there is a general principle governing the actual observance of commandments by women. A distinction is made between positive and negative commandments as well as between those which are time-bound and those which are not. Virtually all negative commandments are binding upon men and women but women are exempt from *time-bound positive commandments.*[14]

> All positive ordinances that are bound up with a stated time are incumbent upon men but women are exempted, but all positive ordinances which are not bound up with a stated time are incumbent upon both men and women; and all negative commandments must be observed by men and women alike.[15]

The time-bound positive commandments from which women are exempt include: the recitation of the *Shema* (the prayer, "Hear, O Israel, the Lord our God, the Lord is One"), the wearing of phylacteries, the wearing of a fringed garment, the counting of the *omer* (a commandment to count each day from the second day of Passover until the festival of Shevuot, the festival celebrating the beginning of the harvest and the giving of the Torah), hearing the blowing of the ram's horn on the occasion of the New Year festival, dwelling in booths on the festival of Booths and taking the palm branch as part of the festival of Booths.[16]

In the matter of cult women are segregated in the synagogue, on the grounds that they provide sexual distraction to men engaged in prayer. They are also excluded from counting in the formation of a quorum (a *minyan*) required for communal worship. Normative Judaism rules that the most sacred prayers of Judaism can only be recited in the presence of "ten free adult males."[17] Nor can women be called upon to recite the blessings before and after the Torah reading in communal worship (to receive *aliyah*).[18] Since all of the functions mentioned are required in communal service it goes without saying that the ordination of women was never entertained.

The legal status of women also excludes them from bearing witness in Jewish courts of law on technical grounds, that is to say, they are not disqualified as credible witnesses but belong to a class of persons whose disqualification is arbitrarily established, e.g., kings of Israel, relatives of the accused (though friends and enemies may testify), etc. The reason for the disqualification of women is not stated but is, in the main, accepted as part of divine legislation.[19]

In this sketch of the role of women in normative Judaism I have focused on those restrictions upon full participation in religious life that have been of primary concern to feminist critics of traditional Jewish norms. These restrictions themselves reflect considerable modification from the severity of the period of formative Judaism as a consequence of the mitigating legislation of medieval rabbinic enactments. But the difficulties these restrictions place upon contemporary women who seek equality in matters of worship, who wish to share fully the rights and duties of communal religious life, are obvious. Thus for example the chief points raised by Ezrat Nashim, a group of conservative and orthodox women, in a manifesto presented to the rabbinical assembly include counting women in the *minyan,* allowing women to read from the Torah in public, allowing women to serve as witnesses in Jewish courts, and allowing women to initiate divorce.[20] The underlying motive for demanding religious and ritual change is not only the attainment of full participation in the spiritual life of the community, but also an enrichment of that life.

In this sketch of the role of women in normative Judaism I have focused on those restrictions upon full participation in religious life that have been of primary concern to feminist critics of traditional Jewish norms. These restrictions themselves reflect considerable modification from the severity of the period of formative Judaism as a consequence of the mitigating legislation of medieval rabbinic enactments. But the difficulties these restrictions place upon contemporary women who seek equality in matters of worship, who wish to share fully the rights and duties of communal religious life, are obvious. Thus for example the chief points raised by Ezrat Nashim, a group of conservative and orthodox women, in a manifesto presented to the rabbinical assembly include counting women in the *minyan*, allowing women to read from the Torah in public, allowing women to serve as witnesses in Jewish courts, and allowing women to initiate divorce.[20] The underlying motive for demanding religious and ritual change is not only the attainment of full participation in the spiritual life of the community, but also an enrichment of that life.

The Holocaust

The effort to initiate social change through a modification of ritual and religious practice cannot be considered apart from the larger theological context and institutional structures which these changes are to affect. While the institutional context is carefully considered, all too often theological issues have been evaded since it has been alleged from the time of Moses Mendelssohn that Judaism is a system of divine legislation rather than a creedal religion. But this is disingenuous. Any examination of the corpus of legislative enactments of the period of formative Judaism and later rabbinic legislation reveals fundamental theological attitudes as well as a larger cultural and institutional frame of reference.

The first response to the holocaust by Jews and Christians alike was silence. But this initial silence has since been replaced by a plethora of historical studies and theological analyses. From this by now extensive literature three theological views have emerged with some degree of precision.[21] First: To be sure, the horror of the holocaust is so overwhelming that it is perfectly understandable to wish to abandon Jewish identity (not to speak of Jewish religious existence) and to merge with the larger world. But to do so would be to accomplish one of the purposes Hitler set out to achieve: the elimination of Jewish life and culture, thus giving to Hitler a "posthumous victory." Second: The traditional values of normative Judaism remain undisturbed since the plan of Providence remains hidden from us. Jews cannot permit Hitler, even in a negative way, to provide the reason for maintaining Jewish identity and practice. There are two variants of the second position. First variant: While we cannot know God's intentions it may be that the re-establishment of a Jewish state is a messianic portent and that messianic times may be preceded by apocalyptic events. Second variant: Even if we could be sure of the eschatological meaning of the Jewish state this would not compensate the victims of the holocaust. Therefore we should adhere to the notion of post-mortem compensation in an after-life in accordance with God's inscrutable intentions. Third: The holocaust is conclusive evidence for the absence of God in history. Either God has turned his face away and has permitted an evil so vast that obedience to his precepts is no longer owed, or his non-existence in any traditionally understood fashion is conclusively established. (These positions reflect for the most part recent existentialist trends; they seem to me to leave open possibilities, still insufficiently explored by Jewish theology, for process, structuralist and post-structuralist interpretations. But these issues lie beyond the scope of this essay.)

The interpretations of the holocaust cited are certainly open to criticism. But there is little doubt that the trauma of the event itself continues to be a predominant factor in the psychological process of Jewish identity formation and a focal point for Jewish (and some Christian) theological speculation. More, the experience of the holocaust can be said to be borne as a kind of "phantasm" by other experiences. There is no experience it does not haunt. It is a negative "trace" that is re-experienced by way of other experiences and gives new meaning to old categories: sin and repentance, exile and return, God's justice and mercy. These themes now require reinterpretation in the light of the community's catastrophe.

The event of the holocaust has created, so to speak, a new kind of Jewish "ecclesiology": a community which includes all those who in actual fact were singled out for the holocaust as well as those who would be chosen on the same criteria should a parallel situation arise in the course of history. Since the holocaust is not the result of adherence to a creed or to a set of precepts, but of the conferring of a historically unavoidable identity, it is a kind of negative grace (the term may be a sacrilege in this context) in a world in which positive signs of divine presence are experienced as lacking. Thus an unbreakable bond is established between men and women upon the basis of this profound but negative "ecclesiology." The dilemma for Jewish women is, therefore, different from that of women in other religious communities for whom full participation in the life of the Church is a primary problem.

Of course it has been argued that while the holocaust is an issue of importance for Jews, still this should not constitute a sanction for relegating women to second class status in ritual life. It is difficult to quarrel with this position. More, every effort should be made to accommodate this pressing interest in a practical way since it stems from the desire to renew the life of the community rather than to undermine it. But if recent historical experience is to be taken seriously it is not possible to compartmentalize these issues. Instead the holocaust can be seen to require the recasting of the term "community." This recasting must be done with sensitivity to the event on the one hand and in terms of a modern theological idiom which reflects contemporary self-understanding on the other. In doing so, we may find that some aspects of recent Jewish theology which the holocaust seems to have rendered meaningless may, in fact, help us to address the issue of the holocaust itself. At the same time we may open up a horizon for the understanding of the difficulties of women whose lives must be lived in its shadow.

Universal Humanity

There is—despite the difference in theological idiom—an underlying similarity in Jewish thought from Moses Mendelssohn to the present: the stress upon ethics. Mendelssohn, the first major Jewish Enlightenment theologian, argues that Judaism is a religion of laws; ritual observance in conformity with biblical and rabbinic legislation establishes obedience to God while ethical legislation regulates the relations between "man and man."[22]

The underlying thread common to modern and post-modern Jewish religious reflection is the emphasis upon interpersonal encounter as the source of moral judgment: other persons are centers of value. The *imago Dei* is to be sought and found in the human being. In fact one could call this position a new natural theology in which the divine purpose can be seen in the form of the demand placed upon us by the existence of others. This form of religious expression is compatible with theologies of radical transcendence but also with radical immanential theologies. The ethical is the domain in which sacred time and sacred space are given expression. The other person is in his or her very existence a part of universal humanity. Sexual differentiation does not disappear in this context but creates a pressure point. If the term "universal" is to be understood as meaning "applicable to each and every existent of the class humanity," then whatever is so applicable, i.e., the demand to consider the other as an absolute source of value, holds for man and woman alike.

In conformity with this point of view a new midrash might be "written" around Genesis 2:18-25. God created Adam. Then he made the birds and the beasts in the hope that a helpmate could be found for Adam. Then he made woman out of Adam's rib, for none of the other living things could be a companion to Adam. *But* God made woman only after he saw that Adam was imperfect. Woman was created to bring Adam to perfection. The creation of woman transforms Adam into universal humanity: man and woman. Since the source of the paradigm refers to

the history of humanity, i.e., pre-Israelite history, its applicabil-
ity can be envisaged as universal: the development of all humankind into universal humanity depends upon the freedom of
woman for its completion. Jewish consciousness lives in the tension of the dialectical relation of the universal and particular.
This tension can be understood in two ways. First: To live the
aspect of *universality* the community must help bring into being
the freedom of man and woman, a universal humanity. To remain true to the trust of *particularity* Israel must remain faithful
to its contemporary experience of the holocaust. The second interpretation of this tension is a reversal of the first: To remain
true to its *particularity* Israel must understand that the concrete
community of Israel, the faith community, is made up of both
men and women. To remain faithful to its *universality* Israel
must recognize that it holds in trust the dark message of the holocaust which is also a message for all men and women.

NOTES

1. Moshe Meiselman, *Jewish Women in Jewish Law* (New York,
K'tav Publishing House, 1978), p. 9. Meiselman's work, while apologet-
ic, provides, so far as I can tell, an accurate account of the sources.

2. *Ibid.*

3. Raavad, Introduction of *Baal ha-Nefesh.* Cited in Meiselman, p.
10.

4. *Ibid.*, p. 40

5. *Ibid.*, p. 34. See also Leonard Swidler, *Women in Judaism: The
Status of Women in Formative Judaism* (Metuchen, N.J.: Scarecrow Press,
1976) pp. 93 ff. For a full scholarly treatment of the Mishnaic period see
Jacob Neusner, *A History of the Mishnaic Law of Purities* (Leiden, E. J.
Brill, 1975) 7 vols.

6. Meiselman, pp. 34ff.

7. *Ibid.*, pp. 125ff.

8. *Ibid.* For the interpretation of impurity as a phenomenon
(briefly treated) see Jacob Neusner with a critique and commentary by
Mary C. Douglas, *The Idea of Purity in Ancient Judaism: The Haskell Lec-
tures 1972–1973.* (Leiden, E. J. Brill, 1973). Mary Douglas' commentary
(the thrust of which is in agreement with Swidler's interpretation) runs
counter to Neusner's historical developmental treatment. It is worth

citing at length in the context of our theme: "The purity rules of the Bible . . . set up the great inclusive categories in which the whole universe is hierarchized and structured. Access to their meaning comes by mapping the same basic set of rules from one context to another" (p. 139). Applying this to the problem of women she continues: "As to all the manifold rules which attribute impurity to women, in menses or childbirth, if in doubt ask the Women's Liberation Movement about the intention to sustain male dominance. And to declare adultery and all improper sex impure, is not that a blow struck in defense of marriage and the family? . . . [But] no one ever said . . . that purity rules were either necessarily effective or the sole instruments of social control" (p. 141).

9. Raavad, Introduction of *Baal ha-Nefesh.* Cited in Meiselman, p. 125.

10. *Ibid.*

11. Swidler, p. 154.

12. Meiselman, p. 99.

13. *Ibid.*, p. 103.

14. Swidler, pp. 83ff.

15. Kid., 1, 7; cited in Swidler, p. 83. (Notre Dame University Press, 1973) speaks of bringing humankind to completion through the creation of woman. Cited in Swidler p. 27. It is interesting to note that anti-semitism and anti-feminism are more than incidentally linked. Where humankind is seen as masculine, womankind is seen as inferior and Judaism's "inferiority" as a religion is then deduced from this. Thus Otto Weinenger, author of *Sex and Character,* writes; "Greatness is absent from the nature of the woman and the Jew." Cited in *The Jew and the Modern World* (ed.) Paul R. Mendes-Flohr and Jehuda Reinharz p. 235.

16. Meiselman, p. 44.

17. *Ibid.*, p. 136.

18. Swidler, p. 92.

19. Meiselman, p. 78.

20. Roslyn Lacks, *Women and Judaism: Myth, History and Struggle* (Garden City, N.Y., Doubleday and Co., 1980).

21. See Moses Mendelssohn, "Jerusalem," in Alfred Jospe (ed.), *Jerusalem and Other Writings* (New York, Schocken Books, 1969) *passim.*

22. The theological literature on the subject is extensive and continues to grow. For a recent overview see Jacob Neusner, "The Implications of the Holocaust," in Jacob Neusner, editor, *Understanding Jewish Theology* (New York: Ktav Publishing House, 1973) pp. 179–195.

HOPE FOR THE FUTURE

Questioning Lay Ministry

Maria Harris

I

As a woman working in both Catholic and Protestant churches, I am often asked the question: "Do you want to be ordained?" My involvement in diocesan pastoral ministry, in seminary education, and in local parishes across the country makes the question a natural one, since most men in such situations are ordained. In recent years, as the churches have addressed the ecclesial status of women more and more directly, I have been forced to articulate a response to this ordination question. In doing so, I have reached the conclusion that for me "Do you want to be ordained?" is not really the question.

Do not understand me too quickly. Clearly, history, theology and the practice of centuries have precluded the ordination of those of us who are women. That is a fact. Clearly, such exclusion has been negatively discriminatory, sexist and unfair. But just as clearly, that same history, that same theology, and that same practice are ineluctably changing. Few theologians today argue for the exclusion of women from ordination (nor should they), and in the course of time it appears likely that women of all churches will join the ranks of the ordained as they have begun to in mainline Protestantism. Those asserting an ethic of full humanity for all can allow no less. That same ethic, however, permits a deeper issue to surface: What is the *form*, the *structure*, and the *shape* the church is to take even if highly selective ordination practices are eliminated? In my judgment, it is this question of church form which is the central one since it points to a division in the church deeper than the one between women and men at the same time it mirrors that division. I refer to the division within the churches of some into clergy and some into "lay." For me, the clergy-lay division, not ordination, is the heart of the matter. In this essay, I will address that division with insights drawn from a feminist perspective.

Clergy-lay as an issue becomes clearer if we examine the changing shape of ministry. "Church ministry is taking on an entirely new shape before our eyes, one that configures much more accurately the symbol of the eschatological people, called in the Spirit, proclaimed in the New Testament."[1] Today's ecclesiology has changed radically to focus on the entire church as a people baptized into mission. The claim to ministry as the work of all Christians is asserted around the globe. Individual churches and individual Christians are realizing that the fundamental successor to the apostolic tradition, and thus to the ministry of Jesus, is the church itself, and that each individual Christian and each individual church must keep faith with the apostles, in contrast to an earlier understanding of apostolic succession as reserved to the papacy or episcopacy.[2] No longer does "the church" automatically mean the ordained, the clergy; no longer is ministry seen as the exclusive work of one group. Such understandings have led to blurred concepts regarding church office, but have not always issued in the realization that crises of office are often crises of ecclesial structures.[3] My conviction is that we face the changing shape of ministry and the crises of office most adequately by addressing the organizational and social relationships in the ecclesial community,[4] especially our organization into clergy and lay. To put it more directly: if all in the church are to claim the work of ministry, the form and shape of the church must be examined, restructured and recreated, and the clergy-lay form may have to go.

Form is not an arbitrary organizational element. Every artist knows that form is not only the *intention* of content; it is the actual embodiment of content. Form is based on a theme; it is a marshaling of materials in relationship to one antoher; it is a setting of boundaries and limits; it is a discipline, an ordering and a shaping according to need.[5] Today the form of the churches in terms of their members has, in my judgment, become elitist: some of us are clergy and some of us are "lay." Perhaps a time in the past existed where this distinction was a positive one and a connotation of "higher" and "lower" did not exist; even if this were once true, I do not think we can make such a claim today. Further, although we have argued for a developed theology of the laity for many decades,[6] the clergy-lay duality itself has remained basically unchallenged. (In one place, for example, Hans-Ruedi Weber himself muses, "I wish we knew more clearly why progress [in lay ministry] since 1945 has been so slow,"[7] without asking whether the very formulation of the issue is getting in the way of accomplishing a new vision of ministry in the church.) A feminist perspective might shed light here. As Rosemary Ruether and others have argued, dualistic thinking—spirit or freedom versus nature, reason versus emotion, soul versus body—has oppressed women.[8] "A revaluing of the so-called negative sides of the classic dualisms and a transformation of the hierarchical mentality are implicit in women's quest. To put it another way, women's quest is for a wholeness in which the oppositions between body and soul, nature and spirit or freedom, rationality and emotion are overcome."[9] In this essay, my suggestion is that clergy-lay borders on being such a dualism, with "lay" reflecting the negative side, especially linguistically, a thesis to which I shall return in a moment. Here let me simply note the division reflected in our images: one is "elevated" or "admitted" to the clerical state and "reduced" or "demoted" to the lay. It pervades our theology: Aquinas in *Summa Theologiae* notes that ordination conveys an active character, baptism a passive character;[10] it limits our vision: problems of/with the clergy quickly become problems of "the church" without consideration of the small number of church members about whom one is actually speaking. In addition to a critique of dualisms, feminism presents a critique of language. "A language is not merely a means of communication; it is also an expression of shared assumptions. Language transmits implicit values and behavioral models to all those people who use it."[11] Feminists, women and men, have learned that they can raise questions about assumptions simply by changing language, and in so doing are (it is Nelle Morton's phrase) "hearing one another into speech." Questioning of assumptions leads in turn to questioning of political structures, including the political structures of churches, and the disturbing awareness that not only are we using language, but language is using us. "We might hypothetically possess ourselves of every recognized technological resource on the North American continent, but as long as our language is inadequate, our vision remains *formless* (italics mine), our thinking and feeling are still running in the old cycles, our process is . . . not transformative."[12] To the way the clergy-lay division and clergy-lay language are concerns for the churches, I now wish to turn.

II

Let us begin with the following principle:

If you have a group half of whose members are A's and half of whose members are B's and if you call the group C, the A's and B's may be equal members of Group C. But if you call the group A, there is no way that B's can be equal to A's within it. The A's will always be the rule and the B's will always be the exception—the subgroup, the subspecies, the outsiders.[13]

Feminists, women and men, have recognized how this principle applies to women and have caused a significant change in language (at least in the United States) by refusing to accept the argument that the generic "man," for example, applies equally to both sexes. But this example is not the only one. People from the United States who spend any time in Central or South America, or in Canada, often begin to recognize the principle in operation when they realize that only one country in the Western hemisphere (their own) uses the term "American" of itself with no qualifier; others are Latin American, South American, Spanish American, Japanese American, etc. Such recognition at least raises the issue of power, and the question of whether a relationships exists between such usage and the fact of being a subgroup, subspecies or outsider. We have, in addition, doctors and "lady doctors," professions and "helping professions," Catholics and "non-Catholics," education (which everyone knows is for children) and "adult education." The list is long, and in most cases illustrates an imbalance of power, suggesting that whoever owns a word owns a great deal more. Finally, there is the distinction fast becoming powerful and prevalent in the churches: that between ministers and "lay ministers." It is this last distinction I wish to examine at some length. Here is the equation:

$$\text{Clergy} = \text{minister}$$
$$\text{Lay, laos, laity (non-clergy)} = \text{lay minister}$$

The words "clergy" and "minister" are, in practice, synonyms; if one wishes to designate as minister a person who is not ordained as a clergyperson, one generally uses the qualifier "lay." The central question this presents is whether one can take the word "minister" and preface it with the term "lay" without at the same time placing the "lay" minister in a subordinate position. (Recall the principle: if you have a group, half of whom are A's and half of whom are B's and if you call the group A, there is no way that B's can be equal to A's within it.) Compounding the issue in this case, however, are the meanings given the crucial words "lay" and "minister" in ordinary speech in the United States. The American Heritage Dictionary of the English Language gives at least three definitions of the *noun* minister: (1) a person serving as an agent for another by carrying out specified orders or functions (e.g., a governmental Prime Minister); (2) a person authorized to perform religious functions in a church—*clergyman, pastor;* (3) a high officer of state appointed to head an executive or administrative department of government. The Oxford American Dictionary offers a similar definition: minister is equal to clergyman; the same is true in Webster's Third New International Dictionary.

In contrast, the *verb* "minister" is not exclusively assigned to any one group: to minister is to attend to the wants and needs of others; to furnish or provide, to give aid, serve; to do things needful or helpful. *Ministry,* the third term in the set, is somewhere in the middle; on one hand, it refers to "the act of serving; ministration" or "the profession, duties and services of a minister of religion"; on the other it is equivalent to "ministers of religion as a group; *the clergy.*"

Examining the word "lay" furnishes more data. The word layman (laywoman is rarely noted) is unambiguous: it refers to "a member of a congregation as distinguished from the clergy," or "one who does not have special or advanced training or skill." Even *laity,* the noun, carries these meanings: "derived from lay (non-clergy)," it means "laymen collectively, as distinguished from the clergy" (women are not noted) and "all those persons outside a given profession, art, or other specialization; non-professionals." But it is the adjective "lay" which is the most telling. It means "pertaining to, coming from, or serving the laity; secular; practicing (psychoanalysis) but not having a (medical) degree" and is from the Middle English *laie,* from the Old French *lai,* from the Late Latin *laicus,* from the Greek *laikos,* from *laos,* the people" (American Heritage). Both the *Oxford Dictionary of English Etymology* and *Webster's Third International Dictionary* begin defining "lay" by asserting what it is not rather than what it is: lay means "not in clerical orders" (Oxford), "not in holy orders; not of the clergy; not clerical; not ecclesiastical" (Webster) and continues "also of or relating to members of a religious house that are occupied chiefly with domestic or manual work" (Funk and Wagnalls call this "menial service"), "not of or from a particular profession," "not having special training or knowledge," "unprofessional," "common," "ordinary." Funk and Wagnalls, besides agreeing with these, adds "inexperienced, ignorant and uncultivated" and concludes with the information that in cards a "lay" hand is one with few or no trumps.

It may be objected here that such usage is mainly for purposes of distinguishing. Possibly. It may be further suggested that no onus ought be attached to manual or menial service. Certainly. But it also may be objected here that such usage, although linguistically accurate, is "only semantic" and not of major concern for the church.My first response is that semantics is never "only." On the contrary, it is the science which deals with meaning, and by definition the meaning assigned to the name of any group is neither irrelevant nor insignificant. My second response is a point made in another context by Paulo Freire: a person who offers such a challenge ignores what can be called the operating force of the concepts and insists on ignoring the real connotation.[14]

However, if one does want to focus on church usage and church practice, many observations are pertinent. To begin with, the ambivalence and subordination built into the term "lay" *is* beginning to be addressed. As early as 1964, *Encounter* published the following: "Every specially ordained minister of the church is and remains first of all a baptized member of the church. He or she continues to belong to the laity, if this term is derived from the biblical use of the word 'laikos,' to belong to God's 'laos,' to God's people."[15] But then the *Encounter* authors make the following notation. "This theologically significant and generally accepted derivation is *etymologically probably wrong.* In the ancient church the term 'laity' was most probably derived from the general use of the word 'laikos' or belonging to the 'plebs,' the common, non-consecrated profane people."[16] I am doubtful in this instance that laity was ever actually used for the entire people; although the distinction between clergy and lay may at one time have had great value, I am unaware from historical study that we have ever used the phrase "ordained laity."

Closer to our own day, the order of Franciscans known as Capuchins in Roman Catholicism have changed the name of their "lay" order from the "Third Order of St. Francis" to the "Secular Order," wishing to do away with not only the implication that the monastic model they live is the sole model of ministry, but also wishing to do away with the centuries-old suggestion that being "lay" is being not in first, nor even in second, but in third place.[17] However, the fact that "lay" is the correlative of "clergy" and thus partner in a divisive pair remains unexamined.

As junior partner in the clergy-lay pair, and as the word which must be added to minister or ministry (as in "lay" minister, "lay" ministry—and in "lay" school of theology for that matter), in order to distinguish it from the *real* minister, the *real* ministry, and the *real* school of theology, the word and the persons so designated are at a disadvantage, rather obviously it seems to me. "Lay" people are the subgroup, the subspecies, the outsiders of Alma Graham's principle. If "minister" without the qualifier pertains to the clergy, to the ordained, then the consequence in the church becomes clerical ownership of a sacred realm, the splitting of the world into profane and secular arenas (another distinction which might be questioned) and second-class status for ninety-eight percent of church people. In actual practice, of course, the correlation of lay and clergy is becoming confused because so many people today exercise the roles of leadership in community and liturgy without ordination. We can go ahead for a long time with the status quo here, but the situation may be telling us something about the way our speaking and the way our formulation of issues get in the way of, and undercut, a serious, positive move which most church people are attempting to support—the participation of all in the church in ministry.

Here let me make one additional set of comments before concluding this section and moving to specific suggestions of advocacy. To this point, I have directed attention mainly to the negative connotations (and denotations) of the word lay. However, when a word is a correlative, or one of a pair, addressing the first has implications for the second. The word "clergy" in Protestantism is synonymous with minister or ministers, while in Catholicism, the word "priest" is still widely used. In my judgment, the present caste system victimizes not only those called "lay," but also those who are ordained, whatever they are called. "They must attempt to meet the expectations of the system and of the community, while holding on to their personal integrity. Maintaining this balance, being all things to all men and women, while at the same time being heroes is a most difficult job description."[18] A change in the language could thus be of benefit to both groups of persons, whether ordained or not, and could lead all in the churches not only to new models of ministry, but to new modes of participation in ministry as well.

How this might be accomplished is the burden of the next section.

III

The following are concrete suggestions offered to those in the church seriously engaged in reflection on the work of ministry. Those who have access to pulpit and classroom, to press and publication, and therefore to articulation and speech in public forums are most especially involved. However, my hope is that not only they, but all ecclesial persons would give serious consideration to these proposals.

1. *Eliminate the word "lay" from the vocabulary of church language, beginning with the term "lay ministry."* The most immediate result might indeed be a certain stiltedness and circumlocution. The fact that no term is readily available is an argument for the urgency of change. A search for more appropriate and equitable terminology is necessary now, before a theology of "lay" ministry is developed. We cannot develop parallel theologies of "lay" ministry and "ordained" ministry; we have to find a single theology of ministry applicable to all. In the past, theologies of service in the church, with the notable exceptions of Congar and Kraemer, have been theologies largely and even exclusively applicable only to the ordained. "Perhaps history is now taking a new turn. What has been on the edges may move toward the center. Such a history would then be written with different views of the church community, and different images of power."[19] Even more important, however, ministry would then begin to be viewed not as a question of office-bearers arranged with more or less authority, but rather as service done within and beyond a local community.[20]

2. *Eliminate the word "clergy" from the vocabulary of church language.* This may be viewed as a move toward "declericalization," but it must be noted that such declericalization cannot be done without the "delaicization" implied by the preceding pages. Ideally, eliminating the term "clergy" cannot be accomplished un-

less the prior conviction is held that ministry is *fundamentally* shared by all the baptized. Eliminating "clergy" might have serious consequences but only "if the non-clergy are willing to move up, if the clergy are willing to move over, and if all of God's people are willing to move out to bear witness to the common enterprise of the gospel."[21] Realistically, it could even mean a re-evaluation of such practices as clerical exemptions from civil service, taxes and lawsuits and an examination of the reasons behind what appear to be double-standard moral expectations with reference to the ordained. These are especially evident in the sexual area, where they range from refusal to ordain practicing homosexuals in some churches to the refusal to ordain practicing heterosexuals in others.

At the same time, however, I would advocate keeping the term "ministry" as the work of the church as a whole, while examining the term "minister" (without the qualifiers "lay" and/or "ordained") in order to see how it is viable. The ancient yet vital terms "priest," "priestly" and "priesthood" may be helpful here, not only from a theological perspective but also for an ecumenical one. Presently, for most Catholics, the "minister" is the Protestant clergyman down the block, whereas for most Protestants the "priest" is that minister's Catholic counterpart. A more careful attentiveness to the corporate dimensions of priesthood and ministry would be an advantage for both churches. Indeed, each of the terms, "minister" and "priest," might even come to have a much broader application for both communions. As Catholics rethink the meaning of ministry and begin to reclaim this language, Protestants might re-examine and reclaim the positive values of priesthood, especially as it is related to mystery, sacrament and community. 1 Peter 2:9 is directed to us all: "You are a chosen race, a royal priesthood, a holy nation, God's own people, that you may declare the wonderful deeds of him who called you out of darkness into his marvelous light."

5. *Name the forms that ministry is taking today.* This begins with the scriptural symbols of the priestly, the prophetic and the political, but it also extends to the forms of service in the world where people live their daily lives. As points of departure,

we might consider the classical forms of teaching (didache), prayer/worship (leiturgia), community (koinonia), advocacy (kerygma) and outreach (diakonia), while encouraging one another, in community, to discover those other areas where ministry is alive. "I think it is being true to our New Testament heritage to suggest that the church must accept and create forms of ministry which will help unite us, that is, the community must perceive what ministries respond to its needs for reconciliation with God by proclaiming the message of Christ."[22] A point to be made here, given the central argument of this essay, is the need for ministry to be *pluri*form and *multi*form, rather than dual in form. Moving in the direction of naming many ministries, we reflect the pluriform Pauline description of the ministries of pastor, apostle, prophet, teacher, helper and administrator, while seeking to be true to the kairos of the twentieth century. "If I could state it as a thesis, I would suggest that the reconciliation of ministries lies in accepting the multiple forms, sometimes even in creating new forms, in response to an understanding of the relationship of ministry to the church and to the person of Jesus Christ."[23]

4. *Examine the nature of ordination, especially from the perspective of its being the precise ritual whereby, at present, clergy become clergy and lay become lay.* Let us ask (a) who is eligible; (b) who decides who is eligible; (c) who does the ordaining, that is, who is the ordaining agent; (d) for how long is a person to be ordained; (e) to what work is ordination directed. As a public issue, such examination is long overdue, and delayed in part because the claims of historical precedent and divine inspiration in raising up candidates have been made with such vigor, and the theology of office and orders so carefully developed. What has not been addressed with similar attention is that, although one *can* claim history and inspiration, the conclusion does not necessarily follow that such divinely inspired historical development is forever normative. Such questions as those suggested above are imperative to a church which claims ministry for all. Still, to this time they have not been universally raised. Perhaps this is because we have no alternate models. Thus our ways of doing things appear obviously appropriate because no other

way of putting things has occurred to us. With reference to ordination, however, other possibilities do exist, and alternate scenarios are being proposed, not least of which are these suggestions of Rosemary Ruether:

> At best, the processes of selecting and educating an ordained ministry should arise from within the self-educative process of the community itself. With trained and committed teachers, the community should be engaged, first of all, in theological self-reflection on its own mission. Out of this process, especially talented and committed persons develop who are designated by the congregation for more specialized training to be equipped to become teachers and pastors (ed.: and many other roles). Ministerial education should be based on the education of the adult community. For more specialized training in theological and social skills, congregations might band together to create schools. The designating of a person as an ordained leader of a congregation (ed.: and other designations) should then be carried out in such a way as to show that it is the community itself which ordains her or him.[24]

Conclusion

My intention in writing this essay has been to raise, at the very least for myself, issues which seem most important for the future of an integral, ecclesial ministry. In no way do I intend it as an *ad hominem* attack on individuals who have given their lives and their persons to the service of God and other human beings. On the contrary, I assume such persons, most of them male, are among those most profoundly aware of the difficulties of church form, and as eager as I to encourage a universal ministry. My own interest, as I have tried to make clear, is with the form, the structure and the shape of the church. I hope the reader will at least take the time to entertain the possibility that maybe, just maybe, some of what is suggested here is correct. Receiving a hearing and engaging in conversation on these issues is valuable, I hope for others, but certainly for me. Beyond this, however, I remain one who hopes that a broader, more inclusive, richer form of church and of ministry may yet be ours; and I remain one who dreams for a different kind of church where all may be one, with neither Jew nor Greek, male nor female, clergy nor lay, but the Christ who will be all in all. The accomplishment of such a hope and such a dream remains, as many feminists have pointed out, a task of naming and transforming symbol and image at the deepest level. Such naming and transforming are catalysts for the birth of a new reality "in which peoples who have traditionally been excluded and invisible are made central."[25] In the birth of a new and chastened language, new myth, and new symbol, we move toward new form and greater wholeness. By doing this we begin to eliminate those forms, structures and shapes of church life which have led, in the past, to division and exclusivity. Questioning "lay" ministry may be a way of beginning such a re-creation in the church.

NOTES

1. David N. Power, *Gifts That Differ: Lay Ministries Established and Unestablished* (New York: Pueblo, 1980), p. 159.

2. Hans Küng, *Why Priests?* (Garden City: Doubleday, 1972), p. 42.

3. *Ibid.*, p. 34.

4. *Ibid.*, p. 33.

5. Ben Shahn, *The Shape of Content* (New York: Random House, 1957), p. 81.

6. See especially Yves Congar, *Lay People in the Church* (Westminster: Newman, 1959); Hendrik Kraemer, *A Theology of the Laity* (London: Lutterworth Press, 1958); Stephen C. Neill and Hans-Ruedi Weber (eds.), *The Layman in Christian History* (Philadelphia: Westminster Press, 1963).

7. Hans-Ruedi Weber, "The Battle Is Not Yet Won," in *Laity Exchange* (The Audenshaw Foundation, 1978), p. 2 (mimeographed).

8. See "Motherearth and the Megamachine," in *Womanspirit Ris-*

ing, Carol P. Christ and Judith Plaskow, eds. (New York: Harper and Row, 1979), pp. 43–52.

9. Carol P. Christ, *Diving Deep and Surfacing* (Boston: Beacon Press, 1980), p. 26.

10. 3, 72, 5.

11. Casey Miller and Kate Swift, *Words and Women: New Language in New Times* (New York: Anchor, 1976), p. xii.

12. Adrienne Rich, *On Lies, Secrets and Silences* (New York: W. W. Norton, 1979), pp. 247–248.

13. Alma Graham, in Miller and Swift, *op. cit.*, p. 32. Graham's formulation originally appeared in a letter to the editor of *The Columbia Forum*, Fall 1974.

14. In *Education for Critical Consciousness* (New York: Seabury, 1973), p. 96.

15. "Christ's Ministry Through His Whole Church and Its Ministers," in *Encounter*, 25, 1 (Winter 1964), quoted in *Theological Foundations for Ministry*, edited by Ray Anderson (Grand Rapids: Eerdmans, 1979), pp. 434–435.

16. *Ibid.*, p. 435.

17. William J. Bausch, *The Christian Parish* (Notre Dame: Fides/Claretian, 1980), p. 110.

18. Ann Kelley and Anne Walsh. "Ordination: A Questionable Goal for Women" in *Women and Orders*, edited by Robert J. Heyer (New York: Paulist, 1974), p. 70.

19. Power, *op. cit.*, p. 83.

20. William Burrows, *New Ministries: The Global Context* (Maryknoll: Orbis, 1980), p. 69.

21. Thomas Gillespie, "The Laity in Biblical Perspective," in *The New Laity*, edited by Ralph D. Bucy (Waco: Word, 1978), p. 32.

22. George W. MacRae, "Ministry and Ministries in the New Testament," in *The Living Light* 14, 2 (Summer 1977), p. 179.

23. *Ibid.*, p. 169.

24. See *New Woman, New Earth* (New York: Seabury, 1974), p. 81.

25. The Cornwall Collective, *Your Daughters Shall Prophesy* (New York: Pilgrim, 1980), p. 98.

From Chauvinism and Clericalism to Priesthood: The Long March

Thomas H. Groome

This essay will, I hope, be read by many people but especially by ordained men. With male clerics as a primary intended audience, I write the following reflections as an ordained male "from the inside to the inside."

The problem of male clericalism, especially as it relates to feminism and the role of women in the Church, requires dialogue at many levels and between many interlocutors. I am absolutely convinced that one arena of conversation is among priests themselves, although raising "the women's question" in the typical rectory or clerical assembly may require some extra courage. The literature on "change agency,"[1] however, makes it amply evident that strategies for changing any social structure or cultural arrangement must include agency for change both from "within" and from "without." This is especially true, I believe, in situations that involve struggles between people who have a certain power and people to whom that power is denied. An analogy may help to clarify this point.

The present situation of clericalism that allows only ordained male members within its ranks and systematically excludes women from ordination and power sharing in the Church is like a fortress under siege. The portal of such a fortress, like all strongholds, has a bolted lock on the inside. Very often the people within believe that the inside bolt is the only one. But there is also a bolt on the outside because the residents within are themselves held bound by their own fortress and hoarding of power. When any one group places itself in "power over" another (and I see clericalism as a "power over" mode of relating or rather refusing to relate), that group is in fact bound by its own oppressiveness. The persons most capable of unlocking the outer bolt are people on the outside. Paulo Freire's contention that the oppressed have the task of freeing both themselves and their oppressors is a powerful statement of this task for those oppressed by clericalism.[2] There is, however, that bolt on the inside of the fortress which needs to be unlocked as well.

Left wing Marxists claim that people in power never willingly let power go from them and that the powerless must take it by force. I agree only in part with their contention. Some pressure from "without" the fortress is essential, and thank God our clerical fortress is now receiving such pressure. But, as a Christian, I am also convinced that by God's grace hearts of stone can be changed to hearts of flesh (see Ez. 36:26); an oppressor/oppressed situation can be transformed without total destruction. For transformation to occur, however, a true conversion on the part of at least some of those "inside" the fortress is required that the inner bolt may be drawn and the powerless may be welcomed. As we do that, we male clerics will be gaining freedom for ourselves as well as freedom for those who are presently excluded from our fortress.

I have long been convinced that any struggle for human freedom is for the freedom of both sides in the struggle. The feminist movement is not just a struggle for women's liberation; it is also a struggle for men's liberation and freedom from the chauvinism that dehumanizes us as it dehumanizes women. Male clerics are gravely mistaken if they assume that the struggle by women for full participation in the Church is something that they can sit back and watch from a distance. We have a pressing responsibility from "inside" to unlock the bolted portico within the fortress that we have built around ourselves, and especially around ordained ministry. The results will be a release for us from the twin captivities of chauvinism and clericalism and a march toward that to which we have been called: the priesthood of Jesus Christ.

The Feminist Journey of a Male Cleric:
My Story

I grew up in Ireland in a rather typical Irish Catholic home and family. As "people of their time," my parents deviated little from the standard sex role stereotypes of husband and wife, mother and father. My father was a politician and a farmer of sorts. He had high visibility in our constituency and was gone from home frequently. My mother stayed home, raised their children, and was his mainstay of support. (It was not very unlike the typical model of political families that persists in American life today.) I went to an all-boys boarding school at age 11, to an all-boys college (also away from home), and, of course, to an all-men's seminary—a process of socialization unlikely to make for a healthy sexuality or attitude toward women. I can't ever remember the question of women's rights in either Church or society being raised.

My first assignment after ordination to priesthood (1968) was to serve as associate pastor of Sacred Heart Cathedral in Dodge City, Kansas. Only then did I realize that there was such a thing as a "feminist movement" (one part of my American culture shock). To the people I worked with in Dodge City, however, the whole movement was a "crazy idea from back east." I also remember the local papers carrying some disparaging stories about "bra burnings" in California. To Dodge City, Kansas this proved our suspicion that California was even crazier than the east. I became convinced that feminism was the latest American fad; it was of no substance or import and would pass quickly (or so I thought). Enough to say that I was not a likely candidate for anything akin to a feminist consciousness.

There were two incidents in my biography, however, that, with hindsight now, had promise of being subversive to my chauvinism. The first occurred in grade school, probably at about the age of nine or ten. One day, an old school teacher was telling the story of St. Brigid, a favorite story in my native county of Kildare since Brigid had founded her monastery at "Coill Dara." Kildare people take great pride in claiming the "Mary of the Gael," as she is called, as their county patron. In the story the teacher mentioned that Brigid's standing was so great in the Irish Church of her time that St. Mel had ordained her a bishop.[3] I remember taking a certain pride in this detail. But the story also stayed with me, at least subconsciously, with the question it had raised for me at the time: "If it happened once, could it happen again?"

The second incident occurred in the seminary in 1964. In February every year, mostly to relieve the winter blues, one member of each class was selected to present a debate paper on a controversial issue to the assembled student body. That year I was selected to present the paper on behalf of my class. Carrying the class colors was a responsibility and the effort was always to outdo the other class representatives in finding the most controversial topic. That year our class won the prize. I wrote a paper entitled, "Arguments in Favor of the Ordination of Women."

I spent a good deal of time assembling my arguments. On the night of the presentation my position was roundly rebutted by one of the "senior theologians" and the assembled student body seemed genuinely convinced that I had received a thorough thrashing in the encounter. To my own amazement, however, *I* was not as convinced that my arguments had been countered. Before the debate I had little personal commitment to the paper's position in favor of ordination, but by the end of the evening I had the gnawing feeling that such a position was in fact a very defensible one. The theological and social atmosphere of that seminary context, however, was far from conducive to pursuing the idea, so I allowed it to drop quietly. I did not come back to it again until some ten years later.

When in 1973 I entered Union Theological Seminary in New York as a doctoral candidate in religion and education, I had a strong interest in the "theology of liberation." In choosing my first semester courses my only criterion was to pick ones with something about liberation in the title or course description. One such course, "Toward a Liberation Ethic," seemed appropriate to my interests. This is where I literally stumbled into my first encounter with a feminist theology (I did not know that there was such a body of literature before then). Only on entering the classroom did I become consciously aware that the course was taught by a woman (Prof. Beverly Harrison), and I was there a good half hour before I realized that women students outnumbered men by about five to one. That course and first semester at Union was the beginning of my struggle toward a feminist perspective.

I can best describe my first real encounter with a feminist consciousness by saying that I went through the five stages of "death and dying" as Elisabeth Kübler-Ross outlines them (denial, anger, bargaining, depression/guilt, and acceptance).

I forgot the precise order in which the stages occurred, but I remembered that my first reaction was "denial." ("This is just a white middle-class movement by women who don't know how well-off they are.") I had my time of "anger." The anger ran especially deep on one particular class day when the women students met with the professor alone and refused to allow male students to attend. Never before had I felt so victimized and excluded. I felt that my rights as a student had been violated as had the academic freedom of the theological enterprise, since this enterprise should include all perspectives in its quest for truth. Only on later reflection did I come to imagine how women must feel about two thousand years of such exclusion. I had my time of "bargaining" with the idea. ("Well I can agree with equal pay for equal work, but something like ordination—ah, the people aren't ready for it yet.") And I remember very clearly my time of "depression and/or guilt." By mid-semester I had an overwhelming sense of my own "guilt" as a man and participation in the corporate guilt of all men for what we have done to women in the world and in the Church. I was "depressed" with the thought that as a man I could not truly be in solidarity with the oppressed—a sentiment that I later, fortunately, abandoned. Finally, I came to a point of "acceptance," not as a point of arrival but as a fledgling commitment and a new beginning. This was due in no small part to the firm but gentle sponsoring of my mentor, Prof. Harrison, whose patience with hindsight now amazes me. By the time I left Union I was thoroughly convinced that "sexism is sinful" (a phrase from a memorable one-line sermon I heard there) and I set myself the task of rooting it out from my own life, from the Church and from our society. I had discovered early that changing one's pronouns is an important but only small first step. The many residual layers of sexism embedded in every male by socialization will take at least a lifetime, and God's grace, to eradicate. But my "long march" had begun.

In the journey since then, I have been especially blessed to have a number of strong women friends in my life who have a deep and mature feminist consciousness. I have been aided little by feminists who tend to objectify evil and place it in males, and subjectify good and place it in themselves. But I have had women friends who did not hate me for being a man and who loved me enough to confront me with my chauvinism when it reared its ugly head—proof of Hegel's point that the most loving thing the slave can do for the master is to rebel. Such a gentle sponsoring approach is essential, I believe, if as the outside bolt on the fortress door is unlocked the inside one is not to be secured all the more tightly.

Feminist minded students have also sponsored my growth in feminist consciousness as have my women colleagues at Boston College. And there have been some male friends and colleagues who have an incipient feminist consciousness; we have helped to sponsor each other. My reading of fine feminist theologians, especially Beverly Harrison, Letty Russell and Rosemary Ruether, has also given impetus to my "long march." Attempting to teach a section on feminist theology in an undergraduate course on the theologies of liberation has placed me in a position (that many teachers will recognize) of interiorizing the truth of what I was teaching. Active participation in the women's struggle (especially through the Women's Ordination Conference and Priests for Equality) has, as participation in the praxis will always do, heightened my consciousness further even as it makes me aware of how far I have yet to travel.

One particular struggle that was something of a catalyst for me was the visit of Pope John Paul II to the United States. I heard with excitement his calls for social justice in the world during the initial days of his visit. But I watched with dismay as the credibility of his stance crumbled when he spoke about the role of women in the Church during the latter days of his visit. In struggling with the clear contradiction between his "domestic" and "foreign" policy I have come to realize that a question like women's ordination is not an intra-ecclesial debate that pales in significance before crises like world hunger and global justice. It is a vital issue if the Church is to have credibility in its struggle with injustice of any kind. It thus pertains to the very heart of the Church's mission to be a sacrament of God's reign. To be an effective sign of God's liberation (the traditional Catholic theology of a sacrament) the Church must first be a credible sign and be seen to be just within its own structures. How can we condemn chauvinism (and all the other sinful social arrangements of our world) if the sin is rampant within our own gates? The pain of having Pope John Paul's call for social justice ignored must spur us on to eradicate the causes of our/ his lack of credibility.

From Clericalism to Priesthood

The confrontation of priests with chauvinism is complicated and made more difficult, I believe, by our clericalism. The fact is that the socializing influences which have formed us have caused us to interiorize twin sources of oppression, namely, chauvinism and clericalism. Chauvinism and a critique thereof is dealt with very adequately in many essays of this volume. I would like to say something specifically about clericalism, again from the "inside."

There are many ways to describe this nebulous attitude called "clericalism." We know it when we see it, but it is difficult to define. Let me begin with some of its typical characteristics.

First, clericalism generally entails an "expectation of preference." The cleric presumes, however unconsciously, that he is preferred in the eyes of God and "by right" expects preference from God's people (especially from "good" Catholics). Second, clericalism assumes a stance of "power over" people, especially in matters religious. Power over it is threatened by anyone who

would question the clerics' authority. Third, clericalism entails
a hierarchical perspective in which clerics see themselves as on-
tologically different from and better than other baptized Christians (the change "for the better" being wrought by the
indelible mark of ordination). As a result the only way to relate
to the non-ordained is "downward." Fourth, because it is elitist,
clericalism binds one to a caste group of fellow clerics. (How often were we told in seminary that our close friends should only
be priests!) As the attitude of a caste group clericalism is inevitably inverted. (The conversation at clerical gatherings is much
more likely to be about "who is getting the next parish" than
about nuclear disarmament.) As an inverted caste group clericalism is self-perpetuating. One joins the closed system, and if a
member faithfully keeps the rules, the rules will keep the member (closed). In sum, clerics see themselves as better than and
different from other baptized Christians. As such the clerical
system is an inherently oppressive one.

Clericalism is the antithesis of the priesthood of Jesus
Christ who came not to be served (Mt. 20:28) and who delegated
his authority only as the right to serve. It militates against authentic ministry in Christ's name, and causes our ordination to
prevent us from living the commitment of our baptism.

My description may sound unduly harsh, but clericalism
deserves to be named for what it is. Not all priests are clerics
and I certainly do not mean to imply that all clerics are mali-
cious or willfully oppressive people. To make such a claim
would be, in fact, to "blame the victim." It is the system of clericalism that I want to destroy. Through the socialization process
by which we are inducted into clericalism, we become the victims of that pernicious system. Clericalism is oppressive to all of
God's people, but it is destructive of the cleric himself. It calls
upon us to play a role rather than to be a person. After that role
model has been interiorized (and our seminaries have been most
effective agencies of such socialization) it is most difficult to "ex-
pel the demon" and become a priest.

As stated above, clericalism is an oppressive stance toward
all of God's people. It takes a unique twist, however, when it is
exercised toward women. There it enters into league with the

chauvinism that most men in our society seem to have interiorized, and the two together now make the last state worse than the first. Clericalism and chauvinism are mutually affirming so that the male cleric finds himself literally in a "double bind" and is thus more securely held bound. An obvious example from our present historical context demonstrates how the two feed off each other.

The present regulation of mandatory celibacy for admission to priesthood tends almost inevitably to affirm and deepen both clericalism and chauvinism. It promotes clericalism by giving the priest a sense of being "different from" and often "better than" other people. But it promotes chauvinism as well in that it easily causes the cleric to assume that women are not only inferior to men but are downright dangerous to one's priestly vocation. Within such a system, authentic human relationships with women become very difficult, to say the least.

It would be unfair to claim that the practice of celibacy by priests in the Western Church is totally without noble motive and purpose. Certainly many people who have the charism of celibacy see it as an authentic one (hopefully they embrace it as one charism among many and not as the one at the top of a hierarchy). But celibacy, as a universal and mandatory law for all who would enter the priesthood, also has its distasteful underside. Its origins are far from free of movements and attitudes in the Church that were rightly condemned as heresy. If we trace its roots back far enough we find that the discipline of mandatory celibacy for all priests is not unrelated to Manichaeism (a heresy of the early Church which claimed that all physical matter is evil). On the contrary, Manichaean attitudes fueled beginnings of the movement toward mandatory celibacy.

Mandatory celibacy as a universal law for all would-be priests is inherently sexist. Not only does it cause men who feel they have the charism of priesthood but not of celibacy to suppress their own sexuality, but it also implies and in effect says to women that their love for such a man could only hamper and hinder his ministry. In that, compulsory celibacy belittles women and in the life of a cleric reduces them further in the hierarchy of clerical values.

What then does such a combined ethos of clericalism and chauvinism call for if we are to move toward priesthood? First, since they express themselves systemically, clericalism and chauvinism demand structural reform. Women must be admitted to their full rights in the Church including the right to priesthood in all its forms (epsicopacy and papacy included). (And I am convinced that priesthood is a "right" to anyone who feels called to it, is prepared for it, and is approved by a Christian community. See Padraic O'Hare's essay in this collection.) Secondly, we must put an end to mandatory celibacy as a universal requirement for entering priesthood. The "long march" from clericalism and chauvinism to priesthood cannot be completed without the presence and full company of women as equal co-travelers. We must struggle for such structural reforms, not be discouraged by apparent setbacks to their realization, and never tire until they are fully achieved.

And even as we look outward toward our structures, we must also look inward and face the challenge of eradicating the interiorized structures of chauvinism and clericalism from our own hearts and personal lives. For us as individuals the movement from clericalism to priesthood calls for a "kenosis," a self-emptying after the mode of Jesus as Paul describes him (see Phil. 2:5–7). Kenosis calls for a letting-go of our elitism and a relinquishment of our "preferred status." Kenosis calls us as clerics to commit "class suicide."

Such an act can truly be called conversion, the kind of authentic conversion that takes the heart of stone and changes it to a heart of flesh. That kind of transformation comes only by the grace of God. It is always God's gift. But in our old Catholic theology we know that grace works through nature and never robs us of our responsibility. Thus, the call to conversion demands that we struggle with, question and critically reflect upon our clericalism, our chauvinism, and their sources. That struggle in turn demands that we enter into authentic dialogue with women of a strong feminist consciousness and dialogue with God in prayer that the grace of conversion may be ours. Only with the conversion of "class suicide" can we march toward what we first felt called to—the priesthood of Jesus Christ.

Some Steps on the Road

Beyond the task and struggle already outlined, I suggest here some more immediate strategies for the pastoral setting.

1. *Mutuality in Ministry*

Moving toward priesthood requires an authentic mutuality with the women who are our colleagues in our pastoral workplace. Given our training and conditioning, this can be a very threatening prospect for many clerics. Mutuality requires a self-emptying (kenosis again) of the elitism of our clerical model to form a new self-identity as "partner."[5] It is letting go of the feigned importance that is typically attached to "what Father says" and coming to cherish and value our own authentic word as it is shared in dialogue with the word of equal partners. While this is threatening to and in fact destructive of our "old selves," it is emancipatory toward our "new selves." It is liberating to realize that we neither are nor have to be the answer person. This is the kind of liberation that comes from the Gospel mode of letting go. Only those who lose their life will find it (see Mt. 10:39).

I am often led to wonder if wearing distinctive garb, especially the "collar," does not prevent such mutuality. (Here I am speaking of the Roman Catholic context at this time in history. Perhaps it constitutes a "surprise element" when women wear it in another ecclesial context. See Karen Bloomquist's essay in this collection.) I am not sure what a "collar" evokes in the typical Catholic, but I suspect that it is more a sign of clericalism than of priesthood. From my own experience, which I do not mean to universalize, I know that it can be a source of clericalism.

Although I had seen it happen to other priests many times, one of the "caste shocks" from my first year in priesthood was the number of "doors" that were automatically opened when I wore the clerical collar. I was treated with a certain deference. I was ushered to the head of the line at banks and checkout counters. Strangers smiled and often said hello. The local drug store would not accept payment for my shaving cream and toothpaste. My bill was often paid for me in restaurants. After some time, I began to realize what such "favors" were doing to my self-identity. I was beginning to believe that I deserved such treatment, that I really was different from and to be preferred to other "normal" people. I recognized this as incipient clericalism. I stopped wearing my "clerical garb" precisely because I wanted to preserve my priesthood—the reason usually given for wearing it. Now I wear it only when celebrating the sacraments in a pastoral setting that seems to make it advisable. (I would not want the priest who anointed my grandmother to have shown up in a suit and tie because of the distraction that might have been to my granny's preparation for death.) Perhaps other priests can wear their "collar" without it leading to clericalism for them, but I found that impossible.

2. *Language*

The task of reforming our language patterns from exclusive to inclusive language is a crucial strategy for transcending sexism. Here the priest, as a public person in the pastoral setting, has a vital role to play.

Many contemporary philosophers of language have brought the importance of this issue to our attention. I have always found Heidegger's explanation of it to be most compelling. Heidegger contends that "language is the house of Being."[6] As such, language names the world within which we reside. But in naming it, language also creates that world and thus establishes its limits and horizons. There is a dialectical and mutually creative relationship between ourselves and the language we use. We create and use it, but our language in turn returns to shape our consciousness and either expands or maintains the parameters of our lives. In consequence, if we continue to use exclusive and chauvinist language, that very pattern of speech will help to maintain us in a chauvinist attitude. We are summoned, therefore, to reform our language. As we do so, our inclusive language will help to reform our consciousness toward inclusiveness and equality.

In everyday speech, in parish bulletins, and in all communication with the people, priests must constantly use inclusive language. But the most pressing arena for reshaping language is in the liturgy and celebration of the sacraments. Anthropologists and sociologists have long ago established the power of symbols to shape human consciousness. In the Christian faith community the most powerful and formative symbols are the liturgical ones. If we use those symbols in an excluding manner and continue to have an all male sanctuary praying in male language to an all male God, then that, perhaps more than anything else, will continue to maintain the Church in its sin of sexism. In the constitution of the sanctuary and its personnel, in our preaching, praying, and reading of the Scriptures, we must deliberately and intentionally structure an inclusive mode of worship that explicitly rather than implicitly includes all of God's people and all of God.

In this task we face a particular problem with the Scriptures. Some feminists claim that the Scriptures are inevitably sexist and have despaired of reforming them to be inclusive. I contend that such is not the case. The Scriptures were undoubtedly written within a patriarchical world view, the world of their time. Thus, indeed, God is most often referred to as "Father" and with male imagery and pronouns. But that patriarchical world view becomes sexist for us only when we continue to be held bound by it and consciously choose to repeat it. We can inherit and preach the message of our Scriptures without repeating the patriarchal world view in which they are couched. Instead of beginning the collect prayers with "O God, our heavenly Father" we can begin instead with "O God, our loving Parent" or with some such phrase. In doing that we will actually be more faithful to our Scriptures and their intention. For while we have shown an undue propensity for "Father" to name God, there are in fact in the Scriptures some fifty images for God, including feminine images.[7]

Shifting from masculine to inclusive language in our liturgy and proclamation of the Scriptures is not an easy task, and the difficulties are augmented by the limitation of the English language. But it is amazing what a little creativity and care can do. After a period of trial and error, we will find ourselves automatically saying that "God made humankind in the divine image and likeness." The "long march" toward an all inclusive language and use of symbols in our liturgy is far from complete but, like all journeys, it must begin with the first step.

One typical objection I have heard raised to such a shift in language is that "the people are not ready for it." Apart from the terrible elitism and paternalism in such a statement, in my experience the claim is just not true. The parish in which I reside can certainly be called a traditional one. On one recent Sunday, the song leader announced that the closing song would be "Faith of Our Fathers." I walked to the microphone and asked the congregation to sing the second verse as "Faith of Our Mothers." I was amazed at the number of positive comments (and no negative ones) I received after Mass, many of them from older women. One grandmother had tears in her eyes as she thanked me and said: "It's about time that our contribution was recognized."

3. *Education*

Beyond the Catholic priest's role in preaching and as president of the assembly at prayer, he also plays a key educational function in the community. Often priests in a parish are actively engaged in religious education programs. Sexism has been rampant in religious education. The priest can render a vital service by calling this to the attention of teachers, checking the textbooks and curricula materials and personally raising consciousness about it so that the educational enterprise of the parish does not continue to socialize people into traditional sex role models.[8] To choose to play such a role is indeed a political choice, but to choose not to play it is equally political.[9]

We also have a responsibility to educate our fellow priests. In that regard I have found my membership in *Priests for Equality* especially helpful. This is an organization of priests who are committed to bringing about the full participation of women in the Church, including ordination. They need our support. You can obtain more information about *Priests for Equality* by writing to: The Quixote Center, 3311 Chauncey Place #301, Mt. Rainier, Md. 20822.

Conclusion

There are many miles left for all of us, myself included, on the long march from clericalism and chauvinism toward priesthood. That journey is as much for our own benefit and liberation as it is for women's freedom. As long as women are oppressed by our clericalism and chauvinism, we are oppressed and dehumanized by our own oppressiveness. Women's freedom will mean men's freedom and ultimately human freedom. As Hegel pointed out, so many years ago, the true self can never be found in the master/slave relationship. As we enter the quest for human freedom for all of God's people, we priests must be prepared to struggle, to read, to question, to reflect critically and to dialogue. This will require a self-emptying, a conversion, a class suicide on our part. We may also be called upon in some circumstances to be what Mao Tse-tung so aptly called a "lived contradiction." We can and must be a contradiction to clericalism and chauvinism even as we live within the present structure of priesthood. In that sense we run the risk of being seen to stand with the community that stands condemned. But the inside bolts on the door of the clerical fortress will have to be drawn by persons on the inside. When that happens, the fortress itself will cease to be a fortress and will become a home where all God's people are welcome. Then the Church will become the Church it is called to be, a sacrament and effective sign of God's reign. And then we too will have become "priests."

NOTES

1. A fine collection of essays on "change agency" is *The Planning of Change*, edited by Warren Bennis, Kenneth Benne and Robert Chin (New York: Holt, Rinehart and Winston, 1969).

2. See Paulo Freire, *Pedagogy of the Oppressed* (New York: The Seabury Press, 1970), especially Chapter 1.

3. Although my teacher did not "footnote his sources" in those grade school days, I have learned since then that this claim can be documented. In Whitley Stokes' *Lives of the Saints* (Oxford: Clarendon Press,

1890) we read the following account of the incident (translated from the ancient Irish *Book of Lismore*):

> Brigid and certain virgins along with her went to take the veil from Bishop Mel in Telcha Mide. Blithe was he to see them. For humility Brigid stayed so that she might be the last to whom a veil should be given. A fiery pillar rose from her head to the roof ridge of the church. Then said Bishop Mel: "Come, O holy Brigid, that a veil may be sained on thy head before the other virgins." It came to pass then, through the grace of the Holy Spirit, that the form of ordaining a Bishop was read out over Brigid. Mac-ceille said that a Bishop's order should not be confirmed on a woman. Said Bishop Mel: "No power have I in this matter. That dignity hath been given by God unto Brigid, beyond every (other) woman." Wherefore the men of Ireland from that time to this give episcopal honor to Brigid's successor.

I am indebted to Mary Condren, doctoral candidate in the B.C./Andover Newton joint program, for this reference.

4. For a classic statement on the history of celibacy see Henry Charles Lea, *History of Sacerdotal Celibacy in the Christian Church* (University Books, 1966, fourth edition). Lea points out that the earliest attempts to make celibacy mandatory for clergy in the Western Church were at the Spanish Council of Elvira in 305. There the deliberations were heavily influenced by Manichaeism (see pp. 23–31).

5. For an excellent statement on mutuality in ministry see Letty M. Russell, *The Future of Partnership* (Philadelphia: The Westminster Press, 1979).

6. Martin Heidegger, *On the Way to Language* (New York: Harper and Row, 1971), p. 63.

7. See Phyllis Trible, *God and the Rhetoric of Sexuality* (Philadelphia: Fortress Press, 1978).

8. See Mariann Sawicki, *Faith and Sexism: Guidelines for Religious Educators* (New York: Seabury Press, 1979).

9. See my *Christian Religious Education: Sharing Our Story and Vision* (New York: Harper and Row, 1980), especially Chapter 1 for a discussion of education as a political activity.

10. For his discussion of the master/slave relationship see G. W. F. Hegel, *The Phenomenology of Mind*, 2nd edition (London: George Allen and Unwin, 1949), pp. 236ff.

The Church of Tomorrow

Richard P. McBrien

The reader should be under no illusions. This essay has not been constructed from ground zero. It is not so much an original piece on the question of women in the Church as it is an application of an ecclesiological perspective to the question at hand. Those who happen to be familiar with my understanding of the Church will not be at all surprised by the context in which this important question is treated. For the rest it may turn out to be a more instructive and illuminating chapter than I could have reasonably expected it to be.

My intention is to situate the question of women in the Church in the context of the total mission of the Church for today and for the next decade. How can we articulate the place of women within the Church's total missionary enterprise?

That question presupposes three other, more specific ones: What *is* the mission of the Church? How, and to what effect, has the Church's missionary self-understanding changed since the Second Vatican Council? What further effects are likely to occur in the near or more distant future?

I should hope that my theological and pastoral explanation will provide a clear and useful context for our on-going reflections on the place of women in the Church, and indeed in society-at-large.

Those of you who have read various articles or heard various presentations on the Church in recent years probably feel that the models approach to ecclesiology has been overdone. Without prejudice to the quality of Avery Dulles' book *Models of the Church*, its unusually lucid character may have induced too many Catholics simply to accept not only the models *approach* as a self-sufficient way of understanding the Church but even to accept Dulles' specific five models as the only possible categories consistent with the approach.

The models approach, despite its overuse in recent years, remains at once theologically illuminating and pastorally useful. It can be especially helpful in clarifying the issue at hand.

When the Church is understood too exclusively as a hierarchically structured institution, with heavy emphasis on the authority of ordained ministers, (Pope, bishops, priests), there is almost no significant place at all left for women in the pastoral leadership of the Catholic Church. Women cannot be ordained and therefore have no real, meaningful access to ecclesiastical authority.

The institutional model insists that the Church's several apostolates are determined and directed from the top. The Vatican or the local bishops have to have the final say in whatever the Church commits itself to publicly and officially.

The mission of this institution includes as one of its constitutive components the responsibility of teaching. The hierarchy, in turn, is responsible for this teaching mission, to be shared, according to their own determination, with anyone else they feel to be competent and reliable. But those who do share in their teaching mission, at whatever level, do so on the hierarchy's terms and at the hierarchy's pleasure. This is the old understanding, for example, of Catholic action, i.e., the participation of the laity in the work of the hierarchy. So even in an area traditionally "assigned" to women, i.e., religious education, women have been effectively excluded from significant leadership roles. If one follows the institutional model single-mindedly, that unfortunate situation is destined to continue.

When the Church is understood primarily as a community—a second major model of the Church—the situation improves. Communities are composed of men and women alike. Community is impossible without mutuality and reciprocity. It is impossible without trust and dialogue. And so, too, is it impossible without a recognition of the fundamental equality of all who participate in it.

On the other hand, the community model of the Church cannot be understood in isolation from the other models, including the institutional. The Church is not just a community. It is a community with a particular tradition and with a particular institutional character. And that is why it is never enough to say that women, for example, should be ordained simply because they are just as much Christian as any man. That is true, but one has to deal with the actual record of the Church's life and experience. One can challenge that record or at least challenge traditional interpretations of it, but one cannot simply ignore it.

Finally, when the Church is understood too exclusively as an agent of social change (the servant model), ever engaged in the struggle for liberation, women can justify their existence within the Church only to the extent that they are thoroughly committed to social justice and human rights and are fully involved in the active pursuit of both. Every other consideration would have to be regarded as entirely secondary to the Christian woman's "call to action." But there is more to mission than liberation.

The nature and mission of the Church, therefore, are not adequately synthesized in any one model of the Church: institution, community, or servant. The Church is all three at once. And its mission embraces the whole range of concerns linked with each model.

The Church exists always and only for the sake of the kingdom of God, i.e., the redemptive and liberating presence of God in the world bringing all things into one, a unity of peace and justice, of love and reconciliation. The Church, like Jesus himself, has been sent to preach the good news of the kingdom in word and in sacrament, to offer itself as a credible sign, or sacrament, of the kingdom here and now, and to use whatever resources it has in the service of those in need and to break down the barriers that remain between the sinful world, on the one hand, and the final kingdom of God, on the other hand, at history's end.

How one understands the place and role of women in the Church will always be in large measure a reflection of how one understands the nature and mission of the Church itself. Or, to put the argument in a formula, as one's model of the Church, so one's understanding of the woman's place and role within the Church.

But the Church in question is not only the Church of yesterday or of today. It is the Church of tomorrow as well. If women are to understand the opportunities that lie ahead, they must anticipate the Church's future course and direction.

I shall review here the principal ecclesiological advances taken by the Second Vatican Council and use them as a kind of benchmark to measure present developments and to extrapolate future trends.

The first and most basic ecclesiological principle at Vatican II is that the Church is a mystery or sacrament, i.e., "a reality imbued with the hidden presence of God" (Pope Paul VI). This principle, articulated in the first chapter of *Lumen gentium*, supplanted the pre-Vatican II emphasis on the Church as means of salvation. To be sure, the understanding of the Church as sacrament was already prominent in pre-Vatican II and para-Vatican II Catholic ecclesiology, e.g. in the writings of Schillebeeckx, de Lubac, Rahner, and Semmelroth. But since the Council it has been recognized as perhaps the most comprehensive way of expressing the reality of the Church.

There are at least two advantages to seeing the Church primarily as a sacrament. First, it reminds us that the Church's mission is not necessarily to bring everyone in, but to establish itself as a visible sign of Christ's presence in the midst of the human community. Second, a sacramental understanding of the Church helps us to see how important Church reform is as a constitutive part of its mission. We must practice what we preach because we have a missionary obligation to manifest the presence of Christ to the world.

I should predict that the sacramental understanding of Church will continue as the dominant mode of viewing the Church, and that it will have increasingly practical, pastoral effects, especially in terms of relating the call for justice outside the Church to the call for justice inside the Church. In the words of the Third International Synod of Bishops' document, *Justice in the World*, "While the Church is bound to give witness to justice, it recognizes that anyone who ventures to speak to people about justice must first be just in their eyes." It will be absolutely essential for the Church, therefore, to be a community where there is full equality not only of races and classes but also of sexes. If the Church is the sacrament of Christ, then it must be clear to all who see it that in Christ there is neither male nor female (Gal. 3:28). The Church projects, for good or for ill, an image of Christ and of the kingdom of God not only through modes of decision-making, through the manner in which it deals with its own employees, through its investments, and through its involvements (or non-involvements) within the larger community, but also in the way in which it respects the fundamental equality of all of its members, women and men alike.

A second major ecclesiological development at the Second Vatican Council is its insistence that the Church is the whole people of God. This principle expressed in the second chapter of *Lumen gentium* replaced the pre-Vatican II emphasis on the Church as hierarchical institution, whereby the study of the Church was more akin to "hierarchology" than to ecclesiology. Pope John Paul II, for example, has insisted in his writings and public statements that the laity do not simply participate in the mission of the hierarchy. The hierarchy assists the whole people of God, to which they themselves belong, in fulfilling the mission which belongs to all by baptism. The "all" here applies, of course, to women and men alike. The statement "We are the Church" can and must be enunciated just as firmly and just as realistically by a woman as by a man. Any institutional or structural arrangement in the Church which fails to reflect that basic theological principle cannot be defended.

A third major ecclesiological development at the Second Vatican Council is the principle that the mission of the Church includes service to human needs in the social, political, and economic orders, as well as the preaching of the word and the celebration of the sacraments. This principle is especially set forth in *Gaudium et spes* and is reiterated in more abbreviated form in other documents of the Council. The principle replaces the pre-Vatican II notion of "pre-evangelization," wherein such service is, or may be, a necessary preparation for the preaching of the Gospel (evangelization), but is not itself essential to the Church's mission in the same way as the preaching itself or the celebration of the sacraments. This may have been the most important ecclesiological development at the Council—namely, the move away from the idea that the mission of the Church is composed entirely of word and sacrament to the idea that the pursuit of justice and the transformation of the world are a constitutive dimension of the preaching of the Gospel (as proposed by the Third International Synod of Bishops). Pope John Paul II's visits to various countries, especially Brazil, Poland, Mexico, and the Philippines, only underscore this ecclesiological theme. The Church, he declared, must "serve the cause of justice" by using its voice "to summon consciences, guard people and their liberty, and demand the necessary remedies." Accordingly, it is the Church's "right and duty" to promote social justice and to speak always on behalf of the poor and the oppressed.

If, even under the leadership of a relatively conservative Pope, this emphasis on the social and political dimension of the Church's mission is destined to continue, then Catholic communities throughout the world will find themselves increasingly challenged and tested in this area. If it is legitimate to ask about the doctrinal sobriety of those who argue in support of the ordination of women, for example, then it is at least as valid to question the doctrinal fidelity of those who ignore the socio-political dimension of the Gospel and the unequivocally strong content of Catholic social doctrine. The Church of the future will have to attend increasingly to orthopraxy as much as to orthodoxy. The call of women to "practice" the Gospel is no less urgent than it is for men. And the call of the Church to "practice" the Gospel toward women is no less urgent for men than it is for women themselves.

A fourth ecclesiological development at the Second Vatican Council is its principle of collegiality. The realization of the collegial principle since Vatican II has been manifested in the emergency of the conciliar process at all levels, but especially in the development of parish councils, diocesan councils, and national councils and/or conferences with bishops. Centralization, while not at all in decline, must at least share the stage with the new stress on local initiative.

The principle of collegiality has implications for the question at hand. If women are full-fledged members of the Church, then they have a responsibility and the right to participate in the formulation of policies and in the execution of decisions. But the formulation process and the execution of decisions emerging from that process must be carried forward in a collegial, not unilateral manner. It goes without saying that women must have equal access to every decision-making body in the Church. For the moment, however, that usually means the parish council, the diocesan pastoral council, national conferences of women religious, and the fulfilling of observer status on occasion at national or international synods. For the future women will be increasingly drawn into the decision-making process at much higher levels, as indeed all laity will be. Women will have to prepare themselves eventually for service in international synods and perhaps someday even in a formal election of a Pope. This is not to exclude the possibility, to be sure, that women themselves will eventually be eligible for election to the highest pastoral offices in the Church.

A fifth ecclesiological development at the Second Vatican Council is the principle that the Church embraces more than Catholics. The Church is the whole body of Christ: Catholics, Orthodox, Anglicans, and Protestants alike. Anyone familiar with the bilateral consultations in the United States since 1965 knows exactly how far in fact we have come since the Council on such major theological questions as the Eucharist, ministry, and even the papacy. It is ecclesiologically archaic, therefore, to use the noun "Church" to mean only the Catholic Church. Catholic women must have the same ecumenical vision when addressing themselves to issues of more immediate concern to themselves. The sisterhood and brotherhood of the Church is more than the sisterhood and brotherhood of the Catholic

Church. Each of us must be open to the witness and experience of other Christian communities, especially those who have already moved forward in permitting women to gain equal access to positions of pastoral leadership. We must inquire into the experience of these other churches to see what effect there has been from the entrance of women into important leadership roles. It is a matter here not only of profiting from their positive experiences but also of learning from their problems and mistakes.

Finally, the Second Vatican Council brought us to see more clearly than pre-Vatican II ecclesiology had that the nature and mission of the Church are always to be understood in the relationship and in subordination to the kingdom of God. This principle replaced what was perhaps the most serious pre-Vatican II ecclesiological misunderstanding; namely, that the Church is identical with the kingdom of God. And if the Church is already the kingdom of God on earth, then the Church is beyond all need for institutional renewal and reform. This may be, indeed, the most fundamental ecclesiological development of this century. Ecclesiology is now done in an explicitly eschatological way. The Church is for the sake of the kingdom of God: to proclaim it in word and sacrament, to signify or sacramentalize it, and to serve it in the larger social and political order. Whatever the Church hopes for is rooted in the promise of God that at history's end we shall be given "a kingdom of truth and life, of holiness and grace, of justice, love, and peace" (*Gaudium et spes*, n. 39).

To say that the Church is not yet the kingdom of God but moving toward it has two important implications for women in the Church. First, we all must recognize that the Church is still short of the mark. It is not yet a community fully transformed by the divine power of reconciliation and healing. We should be utterly surprised, therefore, if we were suddenly to discover a community in which there was full equality between the sexes, the races, different economic classes, etc. So long as we find ourselves in history, on this side of the final kingdom, we shall always be faced with the gap between the kingdom that has been promised and the human situation that we have somehow managed to create. Second, the promise of the kingdom calls us forward in history, with hope and confidence that our efforts here are not in vain. Indeed, the achievements that are evident already since the Second Vatican Council are themselves part of the "initial budding forth of the kingdom," to which the Council itself referred (*Lumen gentium,* n. 5). When we compare the place of women in the Church in the decade of the 1980's with the place of women in the Church even as recently as the decade of the 1960's, much less the 1950's, then we are much less likely to sink into a kind of corporate depression. One looks at a glass and sees that it is half empty, and another looks at the same glass and sees that it is half full. It is a matter of perception. Only to the extent, however, that the Church at-large—men as well as women—continues to commit itself to the struggle for full human rights and for the full equality of men and women in the Church and in society alike can we conclude that there is any substance to this hope.

The struggle for liberation is as much the struggle of men as it is of women. No one suggests that racism is to be combatted by women alone. It is a sin that affects us all and for which all of us are in some measure responsible. On the other hand, women must be ready always to recognize and support those brothers who are willing and sincerely trying to participate in their common struggle. Ironically, and perhaps tragically, the men who sometimes feel the sharpest edge of criticisms from their sisters are those very men who are at least attempting to change the sexist face of the Church. There is a tendency to strike out at those closest to us.

In the final accounting, however, we can be sustained by the conviction that the ecclesiology which has been formulated at the Second Vatican Council and which has been developing ever since will continue to transform the consciousness of the Church at large. As that happens, the highest and most profound aspirations of women in the Church will progressively be fulfilled.

Suggested Readings

Bianchi, Ralph and Rosemary Ruether. *From Machismo to Mutuality*. New York: Paulist Press, 1976, 142 pp.

   The question of sexism in the Church and society is discussed from an historical–theological perspective and from the personal perspectives of each author. Reflections and discussion questions are included.

Burghardt, Walter J., ed. *Woman: New Dimensions*. New York: Paulist Press, 1975, 198 pp.

   This volume appeared as a special issue of *Theological Studies* in December 1975. It is an interdisciplinary approach to insert theology into woman's struggle for freedom.

Christ, Carol and Judith Plaskow. *Womanspirit Rising*. New York: Harper and Row, 1979.

   A collection of essays by some of the finest feminist theologians who investigate our patriarchal tradition, seek to reconstruct that tradition and also search out ways to create new traditions more inclusive of women.

Collins, Sheila. *A Different Heaven and Earth*. Valley Forge: Judson Press, 1974, 252 pp.

   Collins describes the process of doing theology which has led her to "remythologize" religious truths in a way both personal and communal.

Daly, Mary. *Beyond God the Father: Toward a Philosophy of Women's Liberation*. Boston: Beacon Press, 1973, 225 pp.

   In this volume, Daly, a radical feminist, examines the patriarchal symbols of Christianity and their effects on the Christian mind and subconscious.

Daly, Mary. *Gyn-Ecology: The Metaethics of Radical Feminism.* Boston: Beacon Press, 1978, 485 pp.

The three passages of the journey of a radical feminist who has moved beyond *Beyond God the Father* has a great deal to say to women who still identify themselves as Christian.

Elizondo, Virgil and Norbert Greinacher, eds. *Women in a Men's Church.* New York: Seabury Press, 1980, 134 pp.

This volume is one of the latest in the Concilium series. Major topics include historical development, the situation today, theological perspective and new beginnings.

Emswiler, Sharon and Thomas. *Women and Worship: A Guide to Non-Sexist Hymns, Prayers and Liturgies.* New York: Harper and Row, 1974, 113 pp.

The authors provide a rationale for developing non-sexist liturgies as well as examples of such services. Suggestions for liberating hymns and for handling objections to change are included.

Ferder, Fran. *Called to Break Bread?* Mt. Ranier, Md: Quixote Center, 1978.

This book presents the results of a psychological investigation of one hundred women who feel they are called to priesthood in the Catholic tradition.

Gryson, Roger. *The Ministry of Women in the Early Church.* Collegeville, Minn.: Liturgical Press, 1976, 156 pp.

The ministry of women from the first to the sixth century is carefully documented from sources as varied as the Didascalia Apostolorum and Latin canonical texts of the fourth to the sixth centuries. The author concludes, "One thing is undeniable; there were, in the early Church, women who occupied an official position, who were invested with a ministry and who, at least at certain times and places, appeared as part of the clergy."

Kennedy, Ethne, ed. *Gospel Dimensions of Ministry.* Chicago: National Assembly of Women Religious, 1973.

The authors of these essays are concerned with new approaches to traditional ministries and also with the changes in ministry that have occurred in recent years. It is imbued with "a sense of the huge need for liberation of all peoples and groups."

McGrath, Albertus Magnus, O.P. *What a Modern Catholic Believes About Women.* Chicago: 1972, 127 pp.

One of a series aimed at exploring the options opened up to Catholics in the post-conciliar Church, this is a short but comprehensive analysis of sexism in the Catholic tradition.

Raming, Ida. *The Exclusion of Women From the Priesthood: Divine Law or Sex Discrimination.* Metuchen, New Jersey: Scarecrow Press, 1976, 263 pp.

Her research into the juridical and doctrinal foundations of the Code of Canon Law, Canon 968 (which restricts holy orders to baptized males) has led Raming to the conclusion that all the arguments against the ordination of women are based on the assumption that women are inferior to men and that they ought, therefore, to live in a state of subjection. She asserts that law is an essential element in society, but it must be alive, growing and responsive to the needs of people.

Ruether, Rosemary Radford. *Religion and Sexism.* New York: Simon and Schuster, 1974.

One of the first and still one of the best feminist works in the area of religion, this collection of essays investigates the traditional cultural images of women as they have been shaped by the Judeo-Christian tradition.

Ruether, Rosemary and Eleanor McLaughlin. *Women of Spirit.* New York: Simon and Schuster, 1979.

This collection of essays presents a strong picture of the leadership roles women have exerted in Jewish tradition and Christian groups as diverse as Quakers, Evangelicals and modern American nuns.

Russell, Letty. *Human Liberation in a Feminist Perspective—A Theology.* Philadelphia: 1974.

Russell follows the lead of the liberation theologians and claims that the basic teaching of Scripture is a message of liberation. She treats the oppression of women as part of the structure that also involves racism, classism and colonialism.

Russell, Letty. *The Liberating Word.* Philadelphia: Westminster Press, 1976, 121 pp.

This guide is intended for both clergy and laity who are concerned to find ways to make Scripture and worship more inclusive. The authors are all members of a task force on sexism in the Bible (National Council of Churches).

Stuhlmueller, Carroll, ed. *Women and Priesthood.* Collegeville, Minn: The Liturgical Press, 1978, 252 pp.

The faculty of the Catholic Theological Union in Chicago probes the question of women from a variety of disciplines. Their investigation centers on Scripture, laws, traditions and the pastoral psychological dynamics involved in a study of this issue.

Swidler, Arlene, ed. *Sister Celebrations: Nine Worship Experiences.* Philadelphia: Fortress Press, 1974, 58 pp.

This book of sample liturgies (ecumenical, Christian, Jewish) includes some practical advice to women who want to begin developing their own liturgies for meetings or special occasions. It is meant to be an idea book, not to be merely copied.

Swidler, Arlene. *Woman in a Man's Church.* New York: Paulist Press, 1972, 111 pp.

Five essays on such topics as women, the Bible, prayer power and marriage are followed by exercises and questions valuable for discussion groups.

Swidler, Leonard. *Biblical Affirmation of Women.* Philadelphia: Westminster Press, 1979.

A topical review of the references to women in Scripture and in apostolic and rabbinic writings, this book is a very useful reference tool on such themes as feminine imagery of God, women in the Hebrew-Jewish tradition and women in the Christian tradition. Each passage is accompanied by a brief exposition.

Swidler, Leonard and Arlene. *Women Priests: A Catholic Commentary on the Vatican Declaration.* New York: Paulist Press, 1977, 352 pp.

The title says it all. Forty-six essays written by Catholic scholars discuss the Declaration on the Ordination of Women from a wide variety of perspectives.

Tavard, George. *Woman in Christian Tradition*. Notre Dame: Notre Dame Press, 1973, 257 pp.

Besides an investigation of Scripture and the Fathers of the Church this book includes a study of the recent tradition and studies models offered to women by the Christian churches in the nineteenth and twentieth centuries.

Trible, Phyllis. *God and the Rhetoric of Sexuality*. Philadelphia: Fortress Press, 1978, 206 pp.

A volume in the series *Overtures* in biblical theology, this hermeneutical work focuses on Genesis 2–3, the Song of Songs and the Book of Ruth. Trible explores female imagery for God and "the image of God" in human sexuality.

van der Meer, Haye. *Women Priests in the Catholic Church?* Philadelphia: Fortress Press, 1973.

This substantial work investigates Scripture, tradition, the magisterium and speculative theology. Arlene and Leonard Swidler translated the work and added a bibliography and some remarks on the events since the original date of publication (1969).